HOW TO START OVER WHEN LIFE KNOCKS YOU DOWN

Thomas Mietzel

Claim Your **FREE** Gifts And Bonuses…
A $97 Value For Book Buyers Only!

You'll receive:

- ✓ A free PDF of *The 14 Day Real Estate Investor – How To Buy Your First Small Investment Property*
- ✓ A free PDF of this book to share with your friends and family
- ✓ A Lifestyle Redesign Calculator…Learn how affordable your ideal life can be.

Learn how to let go of the past so you can live the incredible future you deserve.

Regardless of the source of your challenges and loss you can recover your self-esteem, rediscover your goals and passions and rebuild your business success.

Let Business and Life Coach Thomas Mietzel put you back on the path to success that is rightfully yours!

Get your free books and Lifestyle Redesign Calculator at:
http://www.TomMietzel.com

SEE WHAT OTHERS ARE SAYING

I thoroughly enjoyed the book. As an entrepreneur and constantly trying to grow your business, I resonated with almost everything Tom talked about. He even goes over his emotional struggle that he endured with his spouse/partner and how he lost his business and revenue, which I completely empathized with. My favorite parts of the book is his candid nature in which he writes it and the summary bullet points at the end of each chapter. Each chapter covered great areas of struggle, most of which deal with mindset/mentality, but in the end you are left with in-your-face inspirational quotes and sayings and words of advice. Awesome read and enjoyed that the author spoke from a position of authority, experience and definitely from the heart.

~ JFo

Reading this book is like sitting across the table from a tough and tender, street-smart guy who's been through it and isn't afraid to tell it like it is. Tom is direct, respectful, funny, and passionate. His story is relatable and easily adapted to our own stories. I felt tougher just reading it. I bought several to give to others. Can't wait for his next book.

~ Janice B

This book will tug at your heart strings and make you think about things in your own life through new eyes.

~ Sheila

Tom Mietzel's book is a "must buy" for anyone who has suffered tremendous personal or professional loss. It is a highly readable and engaging book. The "Final Thoughts" sections for his concise chapters also offer direct and practical advice for readers wanting to apply his tips it to their own situations

- Laura S

HOW TO START OVER WHEN LIFE KNOCKS YOU DOWN
AN AMAZON BEST SELLER

Copyright © 2012 Thomas Mietzel

ALL RIGHTS RESERVED. No part of this work covered by the copyright herein may be reproduced, transmitted, stored, or used in any form or by any means graphic, electronic, or mechanical, including but not limited to photocopying, recording, scanning, digitizing, taping, web distribution, information networks, or information storage and retrieval systems, except as permitted under Section 107 or 108 of the 1976 United States Copyright Act, without the prior written permission of the publisher.

Author: Thomas Mietzel

Editor: Antares Enterprises,

Layout Designer and Cover Design: Heidi Sutherlin

Electronically published in the United States of America

First Edition

FOR THE ONES
WHO PULLED ME THROUGH

I would like to thank a few of the people who supported me during the rebuilding of my life. Without them I am not sure how things would have turned out.

Terry and Connie Timper who are my self-adopted parents. Thanks for the financial and emotional support when I was in serious need.

John and Cheryl Michaud for their friendship and understanding. You don't know what it means to me.

George and Cheryl Schaffner for the help in standing me back upright and being there when things were tough.

Roger and Sheri Schmitt for the lifetime of friendship and all-around concern for me.

Rene Caminatta and Randy Paul for the laughs and emotional support.

Paul and Mary Ann Schmidt and Mike and Ann Schelter for always keeping it real. Nothing like a few beers and good friends to put things in perspective.

Jo Peterson, who made my life in Las Vegas one of joy and fun when I seriously needed it the most.

Steve Schmid, whose funny personality always makes me laugh. Thanks for taking me to Europe when I needed the break.

My Sister Linda Ray and her husband Mike for putting a roof over my head and keeping me fed when things were bad.

My sister Laura Soldner for her soft heart and open mind. Her husband Denny for his genuine decency.

Craig Roeller – Ever since the Marines you have had my back. Semper Fi my friend.

I am not sure how I got so lucky in my life to have these people in my life. Good and decent, loving and caring, supportive yet gently tough, each and every one of them. These and many more have my utmost respect, admiration, and love for sticking by me when things got tough.

If I missed anyone I apologize, but know that you are in my heart and Karma is coming back to you.

TABLE OF CONTENTS

Preface ix

Chap: 1   The Road to Recovery Begins With Faith 1
Chap: 2   Gratitude 11
Chap: 3   Friends & Family 21
Chap: 4   Letting Go of Your Past Mistakes 28
Chap: 5   Letting Go of Guilt and Shame 36
Chap: 6   Letting Go of Hate and Resentment 44
Chap: 7   Forgiveness 54
Chap: 8   Letting Go of Disappointment 63
Chap: 9   Letting Go of the Fear of Failure 72
Chap: 10 Letting Go of the Fear of Success 80
Chap: 11 Lifestyle Redesign 87
Chap: 12 Mentors 98
Chap: 13 Listening 108
Chap: 14 Where Do I Go From Here 117
Chap: 15 The Perfection Trap 124
Chap: 16 Time to Begin Anew 132
Chap: 17 Mental Ammunition for the Tough Days 144
Chap: 18 Resource Guide 154

About Tom Mietzel 158

PREFACE

This is a book for people who have succeeded, and failed, and refused to quit. As you sit, stunned, contemplating your failure and wondering what to do next, it is my hope that my experience may help you get back on your feet sooner than you would have otherwise.

One of the advantages of going broke (something I never would have thought) is the opportunity to push the "Reset" button. When I built my business, I built a business that depended completely on my own efforts. I see now that I didn't really have a business; what I had was a self-created job. For many years I wanted to be important, the one in charge, the "go-to guy." I loved the excitement and pace of the place I had built for myself in life, but what I had done was back myself into a corner where I couldn't grow my business or have any free time. If I didn't work every day to make things happen, nothing would get done. If I went on vacation to get away, I was on my phone or email. I had no life of my own. I built a company that wasn't scalable, a company that wasn't going to provide me with an income for the rest of my life if I somehow removed myself from the equation.

I was accumulating stuff but becoming more and more miserable. When you're able to push the reset button and look at the business and life you built and lost, you can look back with the intent to start over. That leads to a different set of questions than the questions you ask when you're just feeling sorry for yourself. Instead of asking pointless questions like "Why is the universe treating me this way?" you start asking creative questions such as "What did I do right and wrong? Did I build myself a business or a job? Did I have a life or simply an existence?" If you want to rebuild your life and business exactly the same as it was before I'm not here to tell you that you shouldn't do it. But I found, for myself, that what I had created the first time around is simply not for me. I'm 52 years old and have learned the value of time, the fleetingness of life. I want to rebuild my business so that I'm not important to that business, rather a ghost in the machine. I want to build a support system that lets me live and explore life without concern for the day to day minutiae that had previously consumed me. I want a business where titles are unimportant but life well lived is the goal.

The hardest part in starting over is deciding what you want. Do you want the same thing you had, or something different? In my case I liked the business I was in but detested what I had built.

Then I had what seems now to be a stroke of luck: the bankers took me out of the equation by putting me into bankruptcy.

Failure isn't pleasant. It hurts like hell. And the more successful you have been, the more it hurts. But it doesn't have to be the end of your story. If you refuse to let your failure define you, in less time than you may think, you will look back at that failure as the foundation of even greater success.

But that's not where you are today. There may be trials, heartaches, lost friendships and legal troubles to come. If you are like me, your harshest critics will be your own self-doubts. Nonetheless, you may be more fortunate than you think. Once you've cleared the deck of the financial garbage, and your mind of all the emotional baggage, you can think clearly—perhaps for the first time—about what you want to build in the future.

Right now you are probably broke. In simplest terms, broke is a temporary condition we may find ourselves in. Poor, on the other hand, is an attitude which acts like shackles on our future. We see everything through a prism of want and despair and thus have little chance of breaking free from our bondage.

In his book *You're Broke Because You Want to Be*, Larry Winget said it this way: "Poor is a condition I find very sad. Sad, yet inevitable. Jesus said, 'The poor will be with you always.' And they will. There are people who live in societies and countries where there are no opportunities for advancement and it takes all their effort just to survive. They are not going to have enough to eat well or live well and take care of themselves."

Winget continues, "Broke is not a condition like being poor. Broke is a situation you find yourself in because you are either under-earning or overspending." It is present in your life due to the decisions you previously made You must forgive yourself for those decisions and put them behind you.

You see, the difference between broke and poor is all about your mindset. Broke just means you don't have any money right now. I have learned you can still live pretty nicely being broke and millions do it every day. I learned that money comes and goes in your life, but what really matters is your mindset. If you have the mind of a champion, a strong belief in yourself, you will realize that money has nothing to do with who you are as a person. Now, I am not advocating being broke. I just want you to understand that you are not poor.

Poor (if you're not living in an underdeveloped country) is a state of mind. It is a mindset of need without any plan or intention of meeting that need by your own effort. Poor people accept their current circumstances as their lot in life. No money, no car, no home and they assume that is the way it has always been and the way it is always going to be. Poor people develop their mindset around what they currently have or don't have, and give up on their dreams and aspirations, just existing in a mediocre manner.

This book is about the temporary condition of "broke" in which you may find yourself. Do not confuse yourself with the poor. The fact that you even picked up this book should tell you all you need to know about yourself. You may be down, but you're not defeated. You may be broke, but you're not poor. You are a winner in your mind, and that's the place where most of this battle is going to be waged. If you're not quite prepared to believe in yourself yet, that's OK. I will believe in you until you are ready to believe in yourself again. I'm going to have more to say about broke versus poor when we discuss rebuilding your business, your dreams and your life.

As a successful individual, your first instinct may be to just jump to your feet and charge back into the fight. You won't want to spend a lot of time in navel-gazing. That will to action is a good thing, but I want to caution you that you're setting yourself up to fail again if you try to bypass the emotions that come with failure. Trust me—you will deal with those emotions, now or later. The sooner you deal with them, the sooner you can get your head on straight and move forward with clear vision. If you try to ignore them, you'll waste a lot of time and energy in tamping them down, and they'll still be there, smoldering away.

Now let me tell you my story, one loser and winner-to-be to another.

CHAPTER 1:

THE ROAD TO RECOVERY BEGINS WITH FAITH

Our lives improve only when we take chances—and the first and most difficult risk we can take is to be honest with ourselves.

— *Walter Anderson*

Seven years. Seven long years! Working 12-hour days, often attending meetings late into the night, and now I had nothing to show for it but destroyed credit, angry suppliers and bankers, and a self-image that could walk out the door and not even have to open it, slipping comfortably under the door sill. I didn't just feel broke, I felt broken.

It took me a long time and a lot of soul searching to determine where I went wrong, and why I was unable to recover as quickly as I thought I should from my financial losses. Over time, I realized that it wasn't the financial losses I needed to recover from; it was the mental baggage that was holding me back.

I always thought I was honest with myself about my strengths and weaknesses. But it wasn't until I had really hit bottom, when my soul was screaming out for clarity and relief from its anguish, that I did the hard work necessary to admit my deepest fears, regrets and sorrows.

After much soul searching, I found that one of the areas I had to rip out by the roots was my thoughts that I hadn't really deserved the success I had attained.

Before I had met my wife Kathy I had been in and out of a number of businesses. Some had made money, and some had not. When I met Kathy things really seemed to start clicking for me. My friends teased me, saying that I had married a woman richer than me for her money. I didn't think much of it at the time, but when I reflected about this I realized I had been raised to always believe that a man had to make it on his own without help from anyone. But no one can do great things without the help of people around him pushing him up, without the help of a great team.

The people with whom you surround yourself are either going to be the people who push you up or those who tear you down. Somehow I had managed to surround myself with motivated, self-directed and loving people who were pushing me up. At the time, I didn't even realize I was doing it. Now I understand that the only way to be truly successful and happy is to place yourself within the glow of those who wish only the best for you; who speak only the best into your life; who elevate you on their shoulders to push you toward your dreams.

Kathy and I were a great team—in fact, the best team I have ever been on. But then Kathy was diagnosed with Bi-Polar Disorder. In layman's terms, this is a mental disorder that causes huge, unpredictable mood swings. The emotional pain of the deep depressions that come with this disease—both for the person who is ill and for anyone close to them—is almost impossible to imagine if you haven't experienced it for yourself. During one of our first appointments with a psychiatrist, with Kathy sitting right next to me, he candidly told me I what I was in for and told me that if I wanted to leave Kathy I should do so now. He further stated that he and Kathy had already discussed what was coming and what it was going to do to me as well as her, and that she would give me an uncontested divorce if I wanted one. I didn't want one and I told him so. Kathy grabbed my arm and laid her head on my shoulder. She was pleased I wasn't running.

But in the years that followed, the battles we went through together eventually wore me down, and we did divorce. I felt that I had let Kathy down, but the emotional burden had become so heavy that I couldn't carry it any farther. When we divorced things just seemed to stop clicking for me. I had lost my team, I had lost my focus, and I had lost the unconditional love and support that had been pushing me up for all those years. I didn't abandon my dear wife altogether; we continued in contact and might have been on the way to a reconciliation when she died of complications from an operation.

I felt extremely guilty after Kathy died, although I have never admitted it until now. I had left the woman who had been my anchor in life, who had given me opportunities that I may never have had without God sending her into my life. And what had I done? When things had gotten really bad I had run away, afraid for my safety and my financial future. That is a heavy cross to bear, and it has taken me a long time to set it down.

After I lost the most special person in my life, I had a crisis of faith. I had never been overtly religious, partly because I went to a parochial school where religion wasn't sold softly; it was hammered home with fire and brimstone. However, I had always believed in God. I just didn't think him a vindictive, wrathful God as I was told.

When you experience the loss of a loved one it is normal to question, and that's what I did. Actually, my conversation with God began as more of a hate-filled diatribe than a question, but at some point you have to get the agony out of your heart and soul. I don't think God abandons or is displeased with you when that happens. He simply understands it is part of the healing process for some of us.

I couldn't hold the anger in my heart for long; it was simply too exhausting. What replaced it was an emptiness, a void that seemed to consume my energy, my love, and my attitude. Then I found a book on Kathy's table, left there only days before: *The Purpose Driven Life*, by Rick Warren. I still have that book. I will keep it for the rest of my life. It took time, but as the hate receded from my life like a falling tide, I picked up that book and started the long journey back to love and fulfillment, reading the words that had so recently inspired the woman I loved.

Over a year passed. I don't remember much about that year except that it was a year of sadness. Kathy was gone, and the businesses I had worked so hard to build were about to collapse. I needed something to pull me out of my depression, and there was the book. . .

"Laura, I've been reading a bit of the Bible and one of the books Kathy left." My older sister Laura had always been the religious one of the family.

"What did you think?" she asked with raised eyebrows. I think I had caught her by surprise.

"Still reading it, but I read the book Kathy had left cover to cover and I am almost through the New Testament." A light lit up in her eyes.

"I have been praying for this day," she told me. Years before I would have dismissed her comments, but my daily readings had begun to instill a calmness that had been lacking in my life

"I actually watch a pastor on TV," I continued.

I could see she thought I was teasing her. This was more than she had hoped for. "Really," I said when I saw the skeptical look on her face.

"Well, you know, you could go to church," she said.

"You know my stance on organized religion. I'm not a fan." I never bought the idea that going to a church or other place of worship was going to save you if you're a lousy human being.

She sighed, a thoughtful expression on her face. "Well, I am happy that you're finally back on the path. Are you sure you couldn't have taken a longer route?"

"Well, you know me, never one to take the easy way. It's taken awhile, and while I still miss Kathy I know that I will see her again, and for that I can be grateful. When I am feeling down I think of what she would want for my life and it makes me feel better."

What was slowly filling my heart was a sense of peace, of acceptance of what I could and couldn't change in my life. I'm not a fool. I know we all live and we all die. My faith had helped me through the death of my parents with the understanding that they had run their race and had lived a full life. What caused me the greatest anguish was the abruptness of a life lost after a long and heartbreaking struggle to recover. Part of me thought it would have been kinder if God would have just taken Kathy when she first got sick instead of allowing her to fight for years, see the start of a well-deserved recovery, only to be snatched by something else. I felt it was cruel.

Faith is often hard to find in your heart when something unimagined happens. Whether it's the loss of someone you love, the loss of a business or a relationship, or something else, not knowing the purpose of the event makes it difficult to accept. However, the sense of anger and unfairness raging inside me gradually dimmed with the passage of time. I became more reflective, focusing on what those who have passed on before me would want for my life. Would they want me to stay mired in anger, disgust and self-pity or would they want me to think well of them, to remember them with love in my heart and move on?

Ask yourself: what would you want for those you love when you pass away? Would you want them to be miserable and unhappy the rest of their lives, or would you like them to hold their love of you in their heart with all the fond memories of the good times and allow themselves to be happy again? You know the answer to this question for yourself intuitively, and so did I. The question answers itself. I know of no one who wishes ill for those they love after they are gone. Knowing this, why would you endlessly allow yourself to ignore what you know would be their wishes? Are you honoring them by not fulfilling your own destiny? Truly you are dishonoring them by not becoming the best you possible. If you want to do something for them, be happy, be fulfilled, and begin to live again.

It was these thoughts, slowly coalescing in my mind, which helped me to see what my new path would be. Does that mean I don't miss Kathy? Of course not; I always will. What it does mean is that I have accepted the fact that I am not all-knowing and may never know the plan for my life, let alone anyone else's, until I myself cross over. I have accepted that the questions I have will someday be answered—just not today.

As your anger and pain exhausts you, so too will joy for the great fortune in knowing the person you have lost re-energize you. Allow yourself to break free of your pain with the joy that those who have gone before you, and those who are still with you, wish only the best, pray for only the best, and ask only the best for you. Rejoice in the thought that someone has your back in the universe. It truly makes a difference in your outlook and recovery.

If your loss is more business-related, it can be no less devastating. Many have poured their life into building a business, only to see it collapse around them. The hurt and the pain are real, just different from the loss of a loved one. When you lose a loved one there is no going back. What has passed is past and cannot be undone. Other losses can be recovered, can be made better, can be made to serve your life.

Faith is no less important in recovering from financial loss than it is in recovering from the loss of a loved one. As I lost my businesses I had a crisis of faith, but not a crisis of faith in God as much as a crisis of faith in myself. Yes, there were many questions about why I was being allowed to suffer such devastating financial consequences. Why was I being singled out when there were so many others who deserved loss far more than I?

But then I realized that I can't know what is in the heart of those others I envied. I am not their judge, nor do I desire to be. I realized that the universe thought there was a lesson I needed to learn. I was being positioned for a brighter future, if only I was willing to heed the lesson—and try again.

When I reflected on my previous successes I realized that the universe had put the right people and the right situations, at the right time, in my path. I do not believe things just happen randomly with no rhyme or reason. I believe the universe saw that the path I was on was not the right path for me. The universe had once connected me to the right people and situations, and would do so again and again, as long as I had faith in myself. There were bigger dreams and a brighter future ahead, if only I would have the strength of character and the faith in my heart to pursue them.

Rediscover faith in yourself. Rediscover faith in the universe that has shown you the path before. Your loss is simply a stepping stone to greater things in your future. Your challenges are designed to give you the abilities and mindset necessary to achieve even greater things in your life.

As I again began to believe in myself and the benevolence of a universe that wanted me to be happy, wonderful things started to happen in my life. Deals and money began to appear again. New opportunities made themselves apparent. My finances, my health, and my relationships all began to be renewed and refreshed. My previous losses seemed designed to put me on a fresh path of unlimited opportunity if I only dared to accept them into my life.

Faith is the great healer of all losses. Faith in a deity if so inclined, or just faith in a benevolent universe that is in your corner cheering you on to greater things. You may be thinking you are finished, but I am here to tell you you're just getting started. Your future may not look bright right now. You may not know how things are going to work out. Just accept that they will work out—not just kinda sorta, but in the best possible way.

Your obstacles will make you the person you need to be, so accept them as part of your journey; embrace the lessons and forgive yourself. God certainly has.

The second you humbly ask God for forgiveness, you are forgiven. Most of us have already done that, but we are still not making progress. While God has forgiven us, it is often we who have not forgiven ourselves. Without letting go of the past there can be no glorious future, no rebuilt life, no better things ahead. You cannot drag the baggage of the past into your future and expect great things from your life. It is like someone carrying a full set of luggage compared to someone who says "I can buy what I need when I get there." One struggles with much weight and bulk holding him back, while the other travels light and is therefore able to move ahead quickly.

WHAT I LEARNED ABOUT FAITH

- Since religions were set up by man, they are subject to the whims, prejudices and beliefs of man and may not reflect the truth.
- Religion can offer many wonderful things when it focuses on love and forgiveness.
- Not judging is far more effective than judging.
- Imperfection is what makes us human.

- Learning from your mistakes is the goal; punishing yourself for your mistakes is not what God had in mind.
- God doesn't hate you; he wants you to be happy.
- God will give you what you ask for—and work toward.
- If God can forgive you, who are you not to forgive yourself?
- Success is what God desires for you, not suffering.
- Become successful; teach and help others to do the same; live by example.
- Be generous to those truly in need.
- Money is not the root of all evil; jealousy and hatred of those around you is evil.
- Be happy for others or happiness will not come to you.

CHAPTER 2

GRATITUDE

When you are grateful fear disappears and abundance appears.
— Anthony Robbins

"Jeez, I haven't got the proverbial pot to pee in anymore." I was commiserating with my friend Steve over a couple of beers.

I went on, "All those years of work down the drain. Why did I bother?"

Steve is not much of a talker; he was just sitting there listening, causing me to want to keep on speaking.

I was feeling plenty sorry for myself. And, after all, didn't I have a right to? A decade of back-breaking work and all I had to show for it was trashed credit and lawsuits. More and more it looked like bankruptcy was the only way out. "Stupid government and their stupid policies, and the next thing you know business people like us get tossed under the bus. Seems like the only thing growing in this country is the stupidity of those in charge."

More nodding from Steve. Say something, I thought. "What do you think?" I asked.

Steve took his time in formulating his response. I could see the gears working. "Shit Happens," he said finally.

Wow, how profound. Was that all he had to say?

'What do you mean, shit happens?" I asked.

"Lots of people got screwed, you aren't the only one."

Where was the sympathy, the understanding for the rage that I was feeling? I turned with a sigh.

Steve continued. "Not saying it isn't bad, but you're luckier than most." I turned an inquisitive eye his direction. "Most people are morons and are going to have a tough time coming back. You aren't."

I pondered what he had said for a moment, , but my anger had clouded my faculties and I was unable to make the connection. "What do you mean?" I asked.

"Just that most people don't have the skills to pick themselves up. What are they going to do? If they wind up with no job, no home, they will be living under a bridge if they are lucky."

"Heck, I'll be lucky if I am not under a bridge in the not too distant future." I wasn't sure where I was going to be living, but it certainly had me worried.

"Bull," Steve grunted. "You're lucky you have the skills to put it back together. Look, you have friends, a place to live, a car. What are you bitching about? Within a couple of miles of where we are sitting there are probably hundreds of people who wished they had your problems."

Hmm. . . I hadn't really thought about it that way.

"Ya think?" I asked.

"No thinking necessary," Steve said. "I know. It's time to climb down off the cross and get your ass back to work." Steve would never be a literary scholar but he certainly knew how to cut through the veil of whining with which I had surrounded myself.

"Maybe you're right. It could be worse," I said resignedly.

"Damn right. You could be dead, or dumber than you are." Steve smiled his devilish grin. I knew he was yanking my chain now, pulling me out of my funk with his sense of humor.

"Dumb, huh? You looked in the mirror lately?" I said as we began our regular ritual of jokingly insulting each other's lineage.

One of the first steps in your recovery, strangely enough, is to be grateful for what you already have. Are you and your family members healthy? Do you have a job? A roof over your head? Transportation? Food in your belly? Friends who care about you? A family who loves you? An education? A sense of humor? Perhaps you don't have every one of these things. But at a bare minimum, you have the gift of life and intelligence (at least enough intelligence to read and understand the words in a book, or you wouldn't have bothered to pick this one up) with which to seek the things you need and want.

You must realize you are better off than 90 percent of the people in the world. Think of that: nine out of ten of the people in this world would love to have your problems, but here you are wallowing in self-pity.

Over 80% of the people alive today don't have $15 to their name, yet you're worried about being broke?

Gratitude is the magic elixir that starts the juices flowing, that motivates the universe and God to act in your favor, which will ultimately set you up for a comeback. So stop complaining about what you don't have and be thankful for what you do have. Every day, several times a day, speak faith and goodness into your life by thanking God for what you do have.

I thank God for my health; I don't take it for granted any more. There are tens of millions of unhealthy people that would gladly trade it all to simply be able to have their health back; to walk, to breathe without agony, to live without physical pain. If you are healthy and strong, give thanks for that every day. The same is true for your family; if they are healthy, be joyful and express gratitude each and every day.

Do you have a job, transportation, a roof over your head? Sure, the job may stink, but be grateful that you have a job. We'll talk more about finding a career that stirs your passions later, but for now, be thankful you have a paycheck coming in and are able to take care of yourself. You may not be driving the car you want, or living in the place you would prefer, but your car gets you around and you have a comfortable place to sleep. Be thankful, because many don't have those basic things.

Are you eating on a regular basis? That simple thing would mean everything to billions of the world's poor who live without access to sufficient food or even clean water. Thank God every day for the fact that you have food, your children are eating, and neither you nor they are going to bed with pangs of hunger clawing at your belly.

Do you have friends and a family who care whether you live or die? As it is said, "A man with one true friend is truly wealthy." Do you know how fulfilled and meaningful friends and family can make your life? All too often we hear people complain about their family or their friends. I am here telling you to feel blessed that these people are in your life. Accept the fact that friends and family are not perfect, because I have a news flash for you: neither are you. Learn to love them for who they are, be accepting and forgiving of their imperfections, and be joyful around them. You will be amazed how relationships heal and how personal dynamics will change when you are simply grateful every day for those who surround you.

Are you able to learn, to make people laugh, to make people feel special? These are gifts for which you must give thanks. Many people with whom I speak are negative about themselves. They feel they have nothing going for them and no future. When I ask them about themselves—their experience, their interests, their dreams, goals, and education—they will often go on speaking about negatives for long periods of time. They are so close to the problem, their own mindset, that they cannot see the gifts they have been personally granted. Everyone has gifts, and when you take a personal inventory you will be surprised at the things you have that you've been taking for granted. If you still can't wrap your mind around your gifts, contact me (my contact information can be found at the end of this book) and I will forward you some specific techniques to help you get past this mental block.

So each and every day, several times a day, say "God, thank you for my health, thank you for my family, thank you for keeping those I love healthy and strong, thank you that I have a roof over my head, food in my belly and a strong mind that is allowing me to build a wonderful future for myself and those closest to me."

Do this daily and you will start to see your life change. When I was facing my depths of despair this simple technique started pulling me out of my depression. When you are grateful it crowds out the sadness, the regret and the self-recrimination.

Instead of gratitude, I see many people speaking problems into their lives. Remember, the universe is listening, and neither the universe nor your subconscious can discern the difference between your thoughts and reality when you use negative statements about what you are, your current status, or what you can accomplish in the future. When you start any thought or statement with, "I don't want," "I will never," or "I am not," you are unconsciously drawing negatives into your life. Have you ever said "I don't want to have to work all the time," "I will never be rich," or "I am not that smart, rich, handsome, pretty, or lucky"?

Start keeping track of how many times you say that phrase or something similar. Most people speak about what they don't want far more often than they express what they do want. When you say you don't want something the universe is going to deliver the very thing you don't want. On the other hand, when you tell the universe you want something, using the right methods and techniques, you will start to draw it into your life. Remember that using affirmations and speaking about what it is you do want will only work if you back it up with actions. If you tell me you want to be rich yet you're sitting on the couch after a 9-to-5 job, and taking weekends off, I am going to know you're not serious. I wish I could tell you that getting rich is quick and easy. Frankly, it can be quick, but you are going to have to put inspired action into play before anything you say you want in your life is going to appear.

If you are going to make the things you say you desire appear in your life, one of the first things you are going to have to do is imagine yourself as already having attained it. Think about what it would feel like to have that business that sends you a big fat check every month. What kind of house do you live in? What is your spouse saying about you, now that you have accomplished great things, and how do you feel about yourself? What are your friends, your family, and your peers saying about you now that you have risen to great heights? Put as much feeling and vividness into your thoughts of your future self until you can almost hear the wine glasses tinkling, the laughter of your friends and family, and feel the feelings of self-worth that envelop you like a blanket when you are able to share your great abundance.

Let's be clear that I'm not describing an exercise in wishing. It's useless to tell yourself *I wish I was rich. I wish I had a new car, a new house, money in the bank. I wish I was healthy. I wish I could travel. I wish I could do more for my family.* No, as my Grandpa used to say, "Wish in one hand and crap in the other and see which one fills up the fastest." Stop wishing and start seeing it in your mind as already accomplished.

Since this book is about recovering from loss, let's use a few examples of positive affirmations from that particular realm. *I am fully recovered from my loss. I am living a life of abundance. I am in a loving relationship. I am happy. I am in perfect health. I am healthy and strong. I am relaxed and joyful. I am a pillar of the community. I am looked up to by my peers. I am successful in all I attempt. Money comes to me easily. My abundance gives me more choices. I earn more than I can possibly spend. I am debt free. I am enjoying the finer things in life. My family and friends are enjoying the finer things with me. I am donating large sums to worthwhile charities. My wealth continues to grow rapidly and without effort on my part.*

These are just a few examples. Create your own affirmations, by all means. Fill your mind with thoughts like these, and you will begin to see them actually showing up in your life.

Determine the areas of your life in which you would like to accomplish something. Write down what it is you want in a positive affirmation, as if you are already living that in your life. Put it on your mirror or somewhere else where you will see it every day, and speak it aloud daily to start driving it into your mind. In free moments build a mental picture of what each of these areas of your life are like as your future self. Begin to daydream. Live your future life in your mind until it takes on all the reality of an accomplished fact.

You will also need to read books and listen to inspirational material. Turn off the radio and unplug the MP3 player, unless it's playing inspirational or educational material. The radio is simply candy for your mind. If you have a 30-minute commute to work each way you can complete a six-hour educational or inspirational CD course in a just over one week. You're spending time in the car anyway, so why aren't you using this time to improve yourself? If you're not willing to read and you're not willing to use the time you do have to listen to great thinkers, motivators, and inspiring material, then you are simply not going to go anywhere. Don't sugarcoat it; if you are not willing to take steps toward improving yourself then you will not achieve your goals; you will simply die with your dreams still unachieved.

If you don't have the money to buy these courses, go to your local library and get a library card. Many libraries have many of these materials you can check out free of charge. If they don't have them, they are usually affiliated with larger libraries that can order them for you, still free of charge. Many libraries are also online and you can order the materials without even having to drive down to the library to get them. There are also free download sites, like www.audiblebooks.com where you can sign up and download material for free. I recommend you go through these courses multiple times, as you will always get new ideas and inspiration each time you hear them. If you want to buy motivational courses, I would suggest you go to www.nightingaleconanat.com and order the courses that interest you.

Think about this: just using the time of your commute, you can get an education and start building your dreams. Unfortunately, most people won't even take this simple step, and they are destined to remain right where they are: disgusted with their lot in life but too comfortable to actually take the aggressive action necessary to start turning the present state of affairs around to their favor. As Thoreau said, "Most people live lives of quiet desperation."

If you are reading this book you have probably failed, as I have. But you're still here, still willing to fight. The light that is your life has not been snuffed out; it has only temporarily been dimmed. Your light is waiting to blaze to new levels of glory and success. I know you might be scared. Join the crowd! Doing something out of the ordinary is scary. And yes, you may fail— but you have realized that failure isn't fatal; it is at most a temporary detour on what for you is an incredible journey.

Put failure in perspective. Failure isn't fatal, but failure to try is the slowest and most painful way to die! Don't die a meaningless death. When it is time to meet your maker, go out with the knowledge that you gave it your all. When you meet God, which would you rather say: "I gave it everything I had" or "I was too afraid to even try"? The difference between success and failure isn't a mile; it's more like an inch. Go the extra inch and believe in a better future for yourself.

THOUGHTS ON GRATITUDE

- Unless you are grateful for what you have the universe will not grant you more.
- If you think you have it tough, do a bit of traveling in the Third World and you will see what tough really looks like.
- Most of the world would trade places with you in a second.
- A goal is nothing more than a dream with a timeline.
- Stop saying the words "I don't want," "I can't," or "I will never."
- Speak success into your life by speaking of things as if they have already occurred.
- Every day, several times a day, speak goodness and gratefulness into your life.
- Read, watch, and listen to educational or inspirational material every day.
- Turn off the TV and the radio; they are candy for the mind.
- Stop listening to the news in all its forms; it isn't news, it is negativity pumped into your brain (this one step will make you feel better quickly).
- Cultivate selective ignorance; the world won't end if you focus on building your life instead of the problems of the world.
- If you're afraid to fail join the crowd. All of us have fears, but it is those who move forward despite those fears that accomplish great things.
- What will you tell God you did with your life?

CHAPTER 3

FRIENDS AND FAMILY

Love is ever the beginning of knowledge, as fire is of light.
— Thomas Carlyle

I had been frustrated at work for quite some time. When I get frustrated or bored, I eat. Apparently I was really not happy, because I had gained 40 pounds. My personal life was great, but I spent a lot of time at work, with plenty of time to stuff my face.

I worked for a great company that treated me well. Unfortunately I like a fast pace, where my actions can have a direct impact on my income. In the retail car sales business, too much was out of my control. The hours were long, but often I had little to do, just waiting for the day to end. When things were busy it was lots of fun, but when things were slow I felt like my brain was looking for an alternative residence. So I ate.

I knew I had to talk to Kathy about it before I dropped dead of a heart attack, so one evening over dinner I dropped the bomb on her. Of course I had made her a lovely dinner to grease the wheels.

As conversationally as I could, I said, "Kathy, I was thinking about doing something different. I hate my job; it is sucking the life out of me. I hate going to work, it's like my brain has rusted up. It is sooooooo boring."

She looked up from her dinner with a knowing look and asked, "What do you think you might want to do?"

I knew I didn't want to keep doing what I was doing, but I wasn't sure what I really wanted. She could always see right through me if I wasn't being straight with her, so I figured I might as well admit it. "I'm not sure, but I want to own my own business again rather than going to work every day for someone else's dream. What do you think?"

She set down her fork and put her elbows on the table and looked at me. "Well, you really should have something in mind before you do something drastic."

Looks like she thinks I have an answer ready to go. Guess I had better take a swing at something she might bite on. "Actually I was thinking about a franchise. Something that has a good track record."

Always the pragmatist, Kathy asked, "Can we afford it?"

This part I did know since I handled the finances. We were big savers and put away my entire paycheck, which in a few short years had really added up. "Well, we have enough saved to live for a few years and enough for a less expensive franchise. And you have a great job."

She looked up with a coy smile on her face. I could tell what was going through her mind. She was going to toy with me like a cat with a mouse. "So you figure you're going to be a kept man."

Admit nothing, admit nothing admit nothing. Didn't take long for her to pin me down. "No, no—well maybe for a little while, until things ramp up."

She was going to enjoy this too much; I could see it in her eyes. "Well, I know you can do it, but I'm putting you on a strict allowance until you get your business up and running."

"How much are we talking here?"

She lowballed it big time. "I was thinking five dollars per day."

This girl should be doing my job. She is better at sales than I am. I wonder if I can get her to come up some on her offer? "Five dollars a day? That's hardly a latte."

"Well, that will encourage you to get something going, now, won't it?" She certainly had a point on that one, but jeez, five bucks a day?

"I'll starve to death on five dollars a day," I protested.

She was quick with the response. "No, I'll pay all the bills, but you'll have to step it up and make it work."

Maybe this wasn't such a good idea after all. I should have made her something else for dinner, maybe a bottle of wine. . . or two. . .

Couldn't she just eat the mouse instead of batting it around for grins? "Cold baby, cold. Can't we talk about this?"

"Depends on how good you are to me." Ah, the point emerges. Going to have to bring on my A game.

With a smile, I asked "What did you have in mind?"

"Well, since you're a kept man and all, I was thinking. . ."

Kathy did support my decision to start looking for something different. First she wanted me to pin down a business and speak with my boss about a leave of absence while I got started, just to keep my options open. I identified something I wanted to pursue and spoke to my boss about a couple of months off in the winter months, without pay, since we were always very slow in December and January. Unfortunately the company wouldn't do that, so I put in my notice and left.

While I developed the business Kathy was at my side, always a confidante, providing the balance that was needed for my personality. She supported me while I got the business off the ground. She believed in me when I was unsure of myself. She loved me through the good times and the bad.

Friends and family can help or hinder your recovery. It all depends on the attitude of your family and the friends with whom you have surrounded yourself.

When your family is focused on success and you have surrounded yourself with positive, life-affirming friends, the magic starts to happen. Problems that seem insurmountable suddenly become a comfortable challenge. When you have people in your life who cheer your success and want nothing but the best for you, it is easier to accomplish great things. Sometimes it's easier just because that support makes it feel easier.

Often individuals who have grown up around a family business or in a supportive environment can quickly shake off failure. Those who love you understand the role that failure plays in your ultimate success and they give you a not so gentle shove back onto the path of success.

The love and support of family and friends is like gasoline for a car. It's much easier to drive someplace than to push the car yourself. Both will get you there, but one is easier. Successful families and friends do not allow you to wallow in self-pity for an interminable time. They give you a pep talk, a slap on the shoulder, and expect you to get out and try again. If have this kind of support from the people closest to you, count yourself very fortunate. If you don't have that support, you have a big problem.

Studies show you will have the average income of your five closest friends. Your income level and social/economic class are also likely to mirror your family. Look around you. Do your friends have what you want? Has your family achieved the success which you dream of for yourself? If not, I would like to suggest you upgrade your friends and stop listening to your family.

Many times it is our peer group—the people we choose to hang out with—holding us back. That includes family and friends. They do it for a couple of reasons. The first reason is if you succeed and they don't, they will have to look at themselves differently in the mirror. If your friends and family are complaining that there is no opportunity for them, no shot at a better life, and you prove them wrong, what do you think that does to their egos? Frankly, you would be doing them a huge favor by showing them the way, but you can't escape from your current situation when you are surrounded by negative energy. I am a very positive person and I always thought I could make negative people positive. But the sad truth is, negative people drain your energy and attitude and pull you down. You cannot help them from your current position. Now, this doesn't mean you can't love them, pray for them, and wish them all the best. But the best thing you can do for them is to show them another path, and that means leaving them behind. In the case of family that will probably not mean cutting them out of your life; it simply means you chart your own course and stop listening to their chattering voices. They cannot lead you where they have never been. You must follow those who have blazed the path to where you wish to go.

The second reason your friends and family make you feel that you shouldn't try again is more benevolent, but no less destructive. When your friends and family have seen how your mistakes have affected you—your disappointment, your financial challenges—they don't want you to see you go through the problem again. What they don't realize is they are asking you to settle for what is rather than what can be, to leave your talent and abilities untapped and underutilized. They are thinking small, and they want you to think small as well. If you have small dreams, or no dreams at all, you will rarely be disappointed. Imagine yourself as a leaf floating on the water. Without dreams and direction you are simply flotsam washing in the waves, ending up on whatever beach the current takes you. You need to have focus and determine which beach is for you, and grow some arms and start paddling, before your inaction destroys your future.

THOUGHTS ON FAMILY AND FRIENDS

- You become like those you hang out with.
- Friends and family can pull you down or push you up.
- Listen to those pushing you up, ignore the others.
- Love is the fuel that drives you to success.

- If you aren't surrounded by love and support, seek it out with the urgency that a man in the desert seeks water; it's that important.
- Support your friends and family in their mental journey to success.
- Be the friend that believes.
- Be the family member that speaks joy into your family members.
- Don't give up on your family, but don't let them hold you back either.
- Surround yourself with friends you wish to model.
- Your success may be the lighthouse that guides your family to a successful life.
- Help those who want to help themselves, but don't fall into the trap of being an enabler for friends or family members who want to be supported financially when they can work for it themselves.
- Waste little time on those who refuse to help themselves.
- If you financially help friends and family it should be limited and directed toward an agreed-upon goal.
- There is a big difference between a hand up and a handout.
- If people have supported you, be sure to repay them in kind.
- Pick a direction for your life or a direction will pick you.

CHAPTER 4

LETTING GO OF YOUR PAST MISTAKES

Fall down seven times, stand up eight.
– Japanese Proverb

Sleeping pills to go to sleep, then coffee to wake up. During the day I was eating Ibuprofen like they were coming out of a Pez dispenser to stave off the inevitable nasty headache. Pepto Bismol for lunch to turn off the fire in my guts, and another gulp for dinner. Fall into bed unable to shut off my mind, leading to another round of sleeping pills. . . day after day.

One of my closest friends, going all the way back to college, had invested hundreds of thousands of dollars with me, and he wasn't going to get it back. I was eating for comfort and contemplating if anyone would miss me if I simply fell off the earth. I couldn't put it off any longer. I picked up the phone and called my friend John. I told him I wanted to come up and talk to him about the project. I suspect he already knew what I had to tell him.

Typical small talk followed by the words I had been dreading: "John, I'm broke. The banks have called my notes, we can't sell any units since the lake drained... I'm sorry."

I wondered if he was going to punch me out, and as low as I felt I actually kind of hoped he would. Or perhaps back over me in the driveway. It would have been a kindness.

But, wonder of wonders, he wasn't angry. "Tom, people a lot smarter than you have screwed up."

I was stunned into momentary silence. Had one of my lifelong and best friends just called me an idiot, a moron, a dolt? Maybe I was, but my dumbfounded look encouraged him to continue.

"Tom people with huge research teams, investment groups with millions of dollars—everyone has taken a beating. We're still friends."

Tears welled up in my eyes. Was John letting me off the hook? I had just told a dear friend who trusted me that I had lost almost $400,000 of his hard-earned dollars. And he wasn't even going to chew me out?

"John, you don't know what this means to me. I'm speechless." This was not at all how I'd expected this conversation to go. What do you say to someone who is letting you move past your mistakes, who still has your back even after you've cost him so much? How did I get so lucky to have friends like this? The universe must really love me.

"Tom, money comes and goes, but friends are what matters. How do you plan for something like the lake draining? Things broke against us, the government raised rates 13 times, the lake drained and the economy tanked... excrement occurs. Let's make lots of money on the next one."

I sat there in silence, contemplating my good fortune not only in John letting me off the hook but in my unbelievably fortunate selection of a friend. Everything he said was true. Yet even though so many factors had been out of my control, it was still my project lying dead on the floor in front of us. Wasn't there anything I could have done differently?

"You got it, John," was all I could croak out.

In most cultures we are taught that mistakes are bad. If we make a mistake we should be afraid to try again and we should carry the guilt of our failure for a long time. I believe that much of our fear of mistakes stems from our indoctrination in school. From early childhood we are taught that we need to study to learn the right answer. The problem with that approach is that most people learn from making mistakes. That's how we as humans have evolved. When we buy into the idea that we need to have the right answer from the very beginning, as soon as we make a mistake we stop and try to analyze what went wrong. We fear moving ahead because of our desire not to make a mistake, rather than accepting our mistakes with the calm understanding that it's always possible to adjust course as we go.

In school we are chastised and made to feel foolish when we give the wrong answer. But look back a little further. When you were a very young child, did you let mistakes stop you? How many times did you have to fall down learning to walk, ride a bike, or climb a set of steps? Your parents were probably there, encouraging you to make those first steps, helping you learn to ride a bike or climb steps. You were not punished or made to feel small and inadequate. Instead you were encouraged to try again and again, and yet again, until you mastered the skill. Acceptance of mistakes as a part of the learning process is the model we all started with (unless we were abused), and it's unfortunate that the model that works is abandoned so soon. However, once we start school at the age of five or so we are continually dosed with negative reinforcement for our mistakes. Our teachers correct us rather than suggesting we try again, our peers mock us, and slowly we learn that making mistakes is bad. Moreover, we learn that if we don't attempt to answer we can't make a mistake, and thus we don't have to experience the negative consequences of being wrong. Our love of learning is undermined, and our lifetime of avoiding mistakes begins.

After we graduate from high school or college our fear of mistakes continues to grow. We worry about accepting the wrong position, about starting the wrong career, about not getting promoted and moving up in the company. We find new worries every day, all because we fear our mistakes. Keeping a low profile seems to be safest alternative to making a mistake.

Many companies, or individual managers, follow the pattern they were trained to in school by being extremely hard on employees who make mistakes. The result is that employees who are empowered to say yes are far more likely to say no. How many people are fired for saying no? Since no action occurs there is little chance of making a mistake that could risk a negative job report or getting fired. This type of culture tends to develop in older companies that have been around for a long time. Everything has an established procedure and process. As long as you don't vary from the road the company has laid out you are unlikely to make a mistake. If you work for a company like that, I believe you had better begin sharpening up your resume. Old-style thinking like that is going to eventually lead to demise of the company. In this extremely fast-paced world if you're not making mistakes you're not growing. If you're not growing you are dying, and younger, more dynamic companies will arise to take your place.

Entrepreneurial companies tend to be much more tolerant of mistakes because there are not established procedures for every aspect of the job. That means staff are free to develop what works, or discover what doesn't, and their mistakes are chalked up to a growing company learning its way in the marketplace. The opportunity for creative thinkers to do well in this type of environment is far greater than in the archaic old-line companies with their established methods. Mistakes are thought of more as the price of doing business than as the career killer that they might otherwise be.

Government workers tend to be even more risk averse than private sector employees. A government worker can coast through his or her entire career, accepting normal raises, without ever accomplishing anything great or taking any risk at all. In fact, if they take any risks they may create one of the rare instances in which they can be fired. When dealing with government workers in any nation, you are far more likely to hear a no than a yes, especially if the procedure is not well established and requires any original thinking. The method by which one worker passes you along to the next worker so they don't have to make a decision has become almost an art.

If you are an entrepreneur you are bound to make many mistakes. Some of them are bound to be painfully expensive. The key is to avoid the mistakes that can kill your business. You must take risks to grow, and so you will certainly be wrong from time to time. However, if you are right more than you are wrong you will do very well. Once you stop taking yourself and life so seriously you will begin to be able to laugh at yourself and enjoy the process. I have made many mistakes in my business. At some point you need to simply shrug your shoulders and say, "Well, that was a helluva big mistake, all right. Let's try to avoid *that* in the future," and move on.

How many mistakes has mankind made to get us to our current level of affluence? The number is surely uncountable. While many of those mistakes may have been fatal for our forefathers, they are simply gentle taps on the nose for us today. Most mistakes are no longer fatal as they may have been for our forbearers. What is different from past generations is our level of comfort. Even by living a risk-free life that avoids any chance of making mistakes, the average Westerner enjoys a lifestyle of luxury unimaginable to those who lived even a couple of hundred years ago. We can coast through life quite comfortably without having to risk mistakes, or even having to truly think, so most of us do just that. If you want to avoid discomfort, if you want to settle for what life has given you, make the decision to coast, but do so consciously rather than as a fallback position. If you want more out of life it's time to get uncomfortable.

If Thomas Edison had stopped after the first 1,000 attempts at creating a light bulb we might be reading by candlelight today. In order to be great at anything you must be willing to make more mistakes than the next person. Remember: mistakes are our course correction mechanism in life. They are like lighthouses that keep us from going farther into dangerous waters. Embrace your mistakes and move on with calm faith that you are following in the steps of the greatest inventors and thinkers who have ever trod upon the earth. Why be fearful in the company of such men and women? Draw from their example, tap into their strength, allow their challenges and the example of obstacles overcome to inspire you.

Those who are afraid to make mistakes are making a conscious decision to let their irrational fears control their lives. They live their lives in a cocoon of self-denial, believing that they are capable of great things, yet stymied by the very thought of taking action. Those who have tried and failed will often say, "I tried that once, and it didn't work," or "A friend of mine did that, and it didn't work out." That may be true, but they weren't you. Perhaps they didn't have the right skill set, but more likely they didn't approach their new project with vigor and passion. Don't let the mistakes of others influence you. Don't let their failures take away your dream. And don't let your own mistakes keep you from believing enough to try again.

THOUGHTS ON MISTAKES

- No mistakes are bad if they don't kill you and you learn the right lessons from them.
- You are no longer in school, so get over the idea that all mistakes are bad.
- Others have made many more mistakes than you and have gone on to great things—be like them.
- Coast if you like, but at least have the courage to admit it.
- You don't really want to be like those who make no mistakes by making no decisions.
- Be right more than you are wrong and your success is all but guaranteed.
- Be careful of decisions where, if mistaken, you are out of business or a job.
- Be sure the risk is worth the reward.
- If your company punishes mistakes, be worried about the future of your company.
- If your company rewards entrepreneurial risk-taking, the future of your company is strong.
- If you want something great in your life, be prepared to fail until you get it.
- Be happy your mistakes are not fatal; shrug them off and try again.

- Action is necessary to get anywhere, so stop planning and make some mistakes.
- When you do make a mistake, adjust course and keep moving.
- Not dead, can't quit. (old Navy Seal saying)

CHAPTER 5

LETTING GO OF GUILT AND SHAME

Adversity is the diamond dust that heaven polishes it jewels with.
– Robert Leighton

The hits just kept on coming. I had gone from a wealthy man to a pauper in a very short time. I had gone from having a loving wife full of energy to having a wife with severe mental illness. After years of living with her disease I couldn't take it anymore. Ironically, my leaving seemed to trigger a desire in her to return to a normal life, and she had made great strides. I was proud of her and we were very close. She spent all the holidays with my family, and we had dinner weekly and spoke daily. She was coming out of her shell, regaining her sanity, and beginning to flourish—and now this. Kathy lay in a hospital bed, victim of a twisted colon, with a grim prognosis. Friends of ours had gathered, and there was an air of incredible sadness among all of us as I stood holding back the tears, cursing the unfairness of it all.

My sister Linda had been the one to rush Kathy to the hospital. She had called me as soon as Kathy had called her, and I had rushed to the hospital only to find Kathy already in a coma in the emergency room. The doctors told me her colon had ruptured. If I authorized the surgery she had perhaps a 10% chance of survival, zero without the surgery. I wasn't about to let Kathy die without a fight; I authorized the surgery.

"Linda, I should have done better," I said. Linda was Kathy's best friend. They spoke all the time and saw each other often. She was as much in shock as I was.

"You did the best you could. You stuck around longer than anyone else would have." Linda knew the score. She had seen Kathy and me struggle with her mental illness for years. Her words washed over me as the guilt and shame set in. I had always thought there would be more time to work things out, to see what could be again. It didn't look as if Kathy and I would get that chance.

I was grasping for a semblance of a reason, for a purpose, to understand what was happening. Talking seemed to help to vent some of the hurt inside—and the building rage at God and the universe. "Maybe, but if I had been there it might not have happened. How could she not know something was wrong? She looked fine yesterday, a little pale but in great spirits. She was supposed to leave today on vacation to the Bahamas with her mom." And now, instead of going on vacation, she was laying here dying. It was beyond reason.

As each friend appeared the story was retold, reinforcing the surreal feeling, as if it were happening to someone else, not Kathy, not us. "The doctor said it was her medication that made her intestines slippery and that caused the twisted colon. The doc said she must have been in incredible pain and he doesn't know why she didn't come in earlier. He thought it must have ruptured a couple of days ago and that she had to know something was wrong. He said her heart stopped on the table and they had actually declared her dead. When they started releasing some of the gas that had built up in her body her heart started on its own. The doctor said she had a 1% chance but they can probably keep her alive until her mom comes." People nodded and offered their prayers. Where was God? I wondered. This woman has fought for years to recover, and just when she is getting better you do this to her? Where's the justice, the decency, the love?

"Did you call her mother?" Linda asked, knowing that Kathy's mother needed to come quickly.

"I did, and told her Kathy was very sick and she needed to come right away." I looked at Kathy lying on the bed, surrounded by staff working to keep her alive. "I got her a flight, but what am I going to tell her when I pick her up in a couple of hours? That her only daughter isn't going to make it?"

Kathy had been a physician at the hospital where she now lay dying. Her doctor friends all stopped by to check on her as well. In fact, the doctor who did the surgery was one of her friends. Her friends did absolutely everything they could to save her. It was so scary watching all those people around her putting more and more blood into her, adjusting tubes, fussing over equipment. My sister and I stood by her bed, helpless bystanders.

"Her hands are cold. What am I going to do without her? She probably wouldn't be here if she hadn't had that gastric bypass operation to lose weight. She told her friends she wanted to win me back. It never mattered to me that she gained weight from the medications she was on. I just couldn't take the emotional rollercoaster from her bi-polar disorder. After the suicide attempts, I was afraid she was going to take me with her."

"You didn't have any choice. Living with her was getting dangerous. You were very good to her." Linda knew what I was feeling and did her best to convince me that I had been a good husband and friend.

"Maybe, but not good enough. I should have done better."

Kathy's mother arrived at 5 a.m. the next morning. When I picked her up at the airport I told her the news—her only child wasn't expected to make it. We sped to the hospital where Kathy's mom cried at her daughter's bedside. Kathy had been struggling to stay alive and was tired of the fight. Her mother told the staff to let her go, and Kathy passed away quietly.

The funeral was held three days later.

"Tom, Kathy was really lucky to have you in her life. She always loved you." Kay, one of Kathy's best friends, had flown in from Florida for the funeral.

"You took incredible care of her; no one could have done more." Terry, one of our dearest friends, had rushed down to the hospital when he heard of Kathy's problems and stayed throughout the night in our vigil with death.

"You were great to her." "She loved you." "We can't believe you helped her all this time." On and on, her friends and mine stopped by to speak with me and reassured me of my decency and effort in taking care of Kathy, even after our divorce.

It dawned on me that what I had seen as a reason to be ashamed and ridden with guilt was actually an affirmation of love and respect. While I was too close to see it, those around me could. I hadn't failed at all; I had done the best I could with what I knew, and my friends and family saw it. The perspective of those around me was different than my own, and more accurate.

While it didn't happen overnight, I gained a new perspective on the good I had done, on the love I had shown, on the kind of man I really was and that allowed me to let go of the guilt and shame that had threatened to consume me.

When I lost everything it was not my friends or family who were condemning me, it was me condemning myself.

Guilt and shame hold back more people than any other issue. When we fail, not only are we embarrassed by our mistake but we are ashamed of the outcome. Sometimes it is the people around us that heap guilt and shame upon us, but if that's what you've experienced you have to ask yourself: are those the people you should have in your life?

On a personal level I had asked God to forgive me for my mistakes, for the way I had treated the woman I loved, and for my ego-driven foolishness. The Bible says when you ask God for forgiveness he will "remember your sins no more forever."

My friends (my real friends) had forgiven me. My family had forgiven me. God had forgiven me. Why couldn't I forgive myself? In retrospect it may be the cultural norms that I'd been programmed with. I was taught from a young age that mistakes are bad, and if I made one I should be sad for a long time and be afraid to try again. That's a destructive belief, and you need to get it out of your head if you ever want to rebuild your life. Failure is how we learn, and attaching guilt and shame to what should be a learning experience is self-destructive and foolish. You don't need seven years of therapy to get past a failure; you simply need to let it go and put it behind you.

Religious and cultural norms suggest that it is wrong to love yourself unconditionally, that it is ego-driven and makes you a selfish person. But if you don't love yourself, how can you give love to others? And if you don't love yourself, how can you ever feel good about yourself? Self-loathing because of your failures, your looks, or your weight are an anchor around your success. It is OK and even necessary to love yourself. Your love of yourself and forgiveness of your imperfections will make you a much better person, able to give love and compassion to others.

Guilt and shame cannot bring back your loved ones; they can't undo your financial situation. But they can prevent you from moving beyond your present situation to the success that is rightfully yours. Those who would heap guilt and shame upon you for your actions are often covering up for their own failures. They may feel by chastising you, they show themselves that they are better persons than you. It may be true in their minds; it is not the truth anywhere else. The ones who are first to be critical have never been in your position, and were they to be, they would likely handle it with much less dignity and integrity than you.

Guilt and shame are used by others to control you, to manipulate your feelings and your actions for their own benefit. Keep in mind that when someone is trying to make you feel guilty it is more about them and their demons than about what truly has happened. The same tactics have been used for eons, and it is time to stop volunteering as someone else's whipping post.

This is not to say that you should make excuses or close your eyes to your own faults. Never pass up an opportunity to learn what life is trying to teach you. If by earnest self-examination you (only you) decide that you've really done less than your best, take the lessons from that and don't make the same mistake again. Make amends if you decide that's what's right. Determine to do better, and refuse to allow others to dredge it up again. Don't use what you've learned to beat yourself up, and don't let anyone else do that either.

Forgiveness is necessary and closely tied to moving past your guilt and shame. Unless you can manage to forgive yourself your guilt and shame will reflect in your actions and your attitudes and hamper your future success. A humble understanding of what happened and appreciation for the universe allowing you to move into a bright future will serve you much better than self-flagellation.

We are our own worst critics, and it is long past time to simply knock that stuff off. Suck it up, realize you made a mistake (maybe lots of them), and move on. Stop talking about your problems and mistakes as if that will solve anything, and dig out your courage and put it to work to build anew.

THOUGHTS ON GUILT AND SHAME

- Guilt and shame are controlling issues in your mind and need to be kicked to the curb.
- Others who use guilt and shame to manipulate you are not worthy of your time or effort.
- God, the universe, or whomever you look to spiritually has forgiven you; it's time to forgive yourself.
- The world forgives, the world forgets; so should you—move on.
- Loving yourself is a prerequisite to being able to truly love others.
- Stop beating yourself up; there are enough people in the world who will do that for you, and they should also be ignored.

- Guilt and shame are used to manipulate people.
- Don't allow yourself to be manipulated by guilt and shame.
- Don't dredge up the past and don't allow others to do so either; talk about the future instead.
- Understanding what has happened and appreciating the lessons it has taught you does not give you permission to use the past as an excuse, reason, or opportunity to do nothing to recover the good in your life.
- People draw their own opinions; often they are wrong and almost always say more about the other person than you.

CHAPTER 6

LETTING GO OF HATE AND RESENTMENT

You gain strength, courage and confidence by every experience in which you really stop to look fear in the face. You must do the thing which you think you cannot do.

— *Eleanor Roosevelt*

When I was living through the destruction of my personal and financial life I thought I needed a change of scenery. There were too many bad memories where I was, and at the time I thought distance would give me some perspective. I called an old acquaintance and asked if he could use some help in his market area. The market was flooded with foreclosures, and he indicated that he would be receiving many of them and would be able to keep me busy and well paid.

After 14 months, when the business hadn't panned out and I was paying him 40% of my earnings in a market where the average commission was a pittance, I determined to move back home where I knew I could make a living. I had grown to distrust him over his unwillingness to keep his word on other matters. In addition, we had to switch brokerages when he was asked to leave for not following company policy. I could see he was a problem waiting to happen.

I had been working with a client for many months, trying to get them a home that was in pre-foreclosure. We were getting close, but I had a long-planned trip to Europe scheduled and Mark had agreed to keep an eye on the sale.

The buyer decided he wanted to look at another home while I was overseas and Mark wrote an offer on that home and canceled the one I had written, which was due to close shortly. When I returned from Europe he refused to turn the client back over to me, insisting that he would take care of me. I assumed that meant my normal 60% split since that was what I would have earned on the home had he not switched them. When the check came it was for a small referral fee instead of what should have been paid. I cashed the check and waited for it to clear before calling him, since experience had taught me he was the kind of person that if challenged would get nasty. But the call had to be made.

I was nervous when I called but I tried to keep in light. "Hey, Mark, it's Tom. I got the check, but it's short."

I could hear in his voice that he was immediately on the defensive. "What do you mean?"

I stated reasonably in a calm voice, "Well it should have been for just over $7,000 with our 60/40 split, but it's only $2,900. What happened?"

"That's the referral fee," he replied bluntly.

"No, I'm supposed to get 60 percent on that deal. They were my clients."

He retorted with a nasty snarl, "You left them, I found them another house and they bought it, so it's a referral fee."

I was trying my best to remain calm. "I was on vacation. I worked with these people for six months, and just when they are ready to close the short sale you put them in another home and cut me out of the deal. The client said they asked to see the house, you didn't find it for them. You also said that you would watch my business while I was out of town."

As the lead broker the check had gone to him. I had to rely on his honesty to get paid. After working with him I had seen his business style. He was happy to destroy relationships over a few bucks. So I was not surprised at what he said next. "Doesn't matter, I did the work and it's just a referral fee."

I wasn't going to give up that easily. "You didn't do the work. You get 40% off the top as it is. I brought the client, worked with them for six months, showed them over 50 homes, finally found one they liked and you tossed me under the bus." My voice was beginning to rise.

"That's the way it goes. You're lucky to get anything." I was glad I had cashed the check before calling. I knew he would probably try to cancel the check if I confronted him about his actions.

"Mark, you know I need that money, and I earned it. Why would you do this?"

His short, clipped tone was something I had seen him use on other people and it usually did not end well. "I did the work getting them in the home."

I decided to try reason. "When I got back from my trip you wouldn't allow me to work with them, you deliberately kept me out of the loop.

I have the emails telling you I would take over but you wouldn't let me."

"Well, if you don't want the money, don't take it." And there it was. The second I was gone he had decided to shaft me.

I had just made a move, I had budgeted those earnings in to my calculations and I had saved his butt on a home his wife owned, covering for him when he was unavailable. I wanted my money. "What am I supposed to do? We were going to open another location together here in Wisconsin. How can I trust you when you stiff me on my deal? And what about your home in Wisconsin I helped you get short sold? Are you going to pay me on that?"

"You didn't sell it."

I thought, *maybe he will see reason on this. He has to remember the conversations we had about paying me to help get this thing through.* "I ran that short sale from beginning to end and you promised me a referral fee on that for the help."

"Well, we didn't make any money on the deal, so there was none to pay you."

I should have figured this was coming, given how I had seen him treat and speak about others. It was always going to be about the money—his money. He would never tolerate anyone else making a buck that he could grab for himself.

"So your word isn't worth anything," I said, hoping to play on his sense of morality. But that would have required morals to be part of his makeup.

With all the sarcasm Mark could muster, he told me, "If you don't like it that's too bad. I run the show and that's just the way it is going to be."

I thought to myself, good thing he confirmed my nagging suspicions and the suspicions of my friend Jo who had been warning me for months about this guy. This may cost me a few bucks but it is a lot less than getting into business with him and later finding out how untrustworthy he is. "Well that isn't going to fly. I can't work with a guy who cuts me out of the deal with my own client and then refuses to pay me when I do him a huge favor on his own home. If you're not going to pay me what you owe me we won't be able to work together down the road." Not that I had any intention of ever working with him again after this, but I figured I would give it one more shot.

"Guess not." A dial tone informed me that the call had ended.

I never did work with Mark again. I filed a couple of small claims actions against him and the supervising brokerage, but he kept changing brokers, which made it impossible to collect. He also made a number of threats against me. I quickly realized that the grief I would receive trying to pursue a slippery critter like Mark would impact the positive attitude I would need to successfully rebuild my business, so I dropped the lawsuits and let it go.

People like Mark go through life dumping all over people who might have been friends and allies. They eventually develop a reputation that prevents them from ever achieving great success, since in the long run you only get ahead by building solid relationships with other people. You must stay away from poisonous people lest you become like them. Experiences like this one give you an insight into the character of the person you're dealing with. Consider it money well spent to learn the truth about a person before you are too deeply involved with them.

In many ways I pity people like Mark who believe others must lose in order for them to win. Had Mark paid me what he should have he would have made several times that amount just on the sales I made in the next 12 months. I now laugh at how he felt he beat me when in reality he cost himself a fortune.

Self-pity and jealousy are twin poisons closely intertwined with hate and resentment. We are angry at the other person for what they have done to us. But what have they really done to us except to shine a light into our soul, our thoughts, and our past? Our regrets cause us to feel sorry for ourselves. When we feel sorry for ourselves we are mired in quicksand. We speak of how poorly we were treated to everyone we can. Every time we speak of our hate and disappointment, we drive it ever further into our psyche, and into the very essence of who we are. That enhanced feeling of self-pity fosters more hate and resentment, on and on in a feedback loop of negativity. Unless you break the cycle you will only attract other haters into your life. Positive people will flee from you as if you are diseased—which you are. You have the disease of negativism, and it is contagious to those around you. Your negative view of the world and how unfairly you've been treated guarantees that further situations will enter your life to give you more opportunities to be filled with hate and consumed by resentment.

As for jealousy, it's natural to be a bit envious when someone has accomplished more than we have. That only becomes jealousy when you blame someone who is successful for your lack of accomplishment. Some politicians (I don't really need to name names here, do I?) are great at perpetuating the myth that those who have accomplished great things in business or life have somehow gotten their success illegitimately. They are nothing but demagogues using those feelings to manipulate the electorate to further their own selfish interest. If you find yourself in agreement with them, you may need more help than you can find in this book. Get in touch with a psychiatrist right away.

When you are jealous of others you wish bad things for their life. And since karma is fair, what you wish upon another is returned to you doubly. If you want to put the demons in your head to rest, be happy for those who have accomplished much. If you desire to have what they already have, use them as a model of what to do.

Ask yourself: when you hate, does it hurt the other person or does it hurt you? Does your dwelling on your hatred affect the other person's paycheck? Does it affect the other person's relationships that you hold hate and resentment in your heart? It does not. What it truly does is poison your soul.

Think of your mind as a factory. You have an unlimited manufacturing capacity with lots of incredible machinery, but are you turning out weapons of war and destruction or of love and peace? You can't produce both in the same factory, and you need to decide what is more important to you, allowing your factory's output to be consumed by destruction or to using your factory to bring about good in the world and in your life.

When my financial situation went bad, I went back to my old partners and acquaintances to whom I had loaned money in good faith. Do you know, not one of them paid me back? I sued one of my old associates and won, but I was never able to collect so much as a dime. If people are going to cheat you that's just how it is. It doesn't say anything bad about you, but it says volumes about the other person. Unless an enormous amount of money is at stake, my advice is to let it go and move on. Never do business or provide financial help to that person again, but put your loss out of your mind and move ahead.

Believe me when I say there was lots of hate and resentment brewing inside me. It seemed that all my pent-up frustrations, anger, and dissatisfaction were focused on these people who had wronged me. However, I quickly realized that they were simply playing out their part in the drama of my life. I was struggling and grasping for any lifeline I could find. When I realized what I was doing I set the hatred aside, realizing that God, the universe, karma—choose your own name for it—would provide for me and make it up to me down the road.

When you set down the hatred it is an almost indescribable relief. I know people who hate someone who they feel did them wrong decades ago. How much energy has been consumed in the maintenance of that hatred and resentment that could have been used for good? Don't be one of those people. Be a bigger person and realize that there will be setbacks in your life, there will be people who hurt you both financially and emotionally. Pity them, but don't let hatred for them get down inside your soul, or you will become like them.

The great thinkers all seem to agree that hatred is a leash holding you close to the object of your hatred. Anger and resentment can consume all of your mental energy, leaving you nothing to use to build an incredible life for yourself. You are like a magnet attracting into your life what you think about during the day. If you think about how angry you are you will attract more anger and negativity into your life. If you have gratitude for what you do have your thoughts will attract more positive energy into your life.

The first step on your journey is to be grateful for what you do have. It needn't be much—a roof over your head, a car that works, your health. When you start to be grateful for the little things in life you will gradually begin to crowd out the hate and resentment. You cannot simultaneously hold both hate and gratitude in your heart. The more gratitude you hold in your heart the more your hate will weaken. This will require a conscious and concerted effort on your part, especially if you have been filled with rage for a long time.

Second, you need to stop giving your hate and resentment a voice. Speaking of your misfortune will draw other misfortune into your life. Have you ever known someone who is constantly negative? Nothing good seems to happen to them, does it? Is that person you? When you stop speaking of hate and resentment, those feelings will gradually lose their power over you.

It has been truly said that living well is the best revenge. If others have hurt you, do better without them—in fact, do incredibly well. If others have cheated you, make lots of money and leave them in your dust. As you focus on achievement in whatever field you desire, the negative thoughts and feelings will leave you for more fertile ground in smaller souls, and you will be left only with a field of opportunity in which to play.

THOUGHTS ON HATE AND RESENTMENT

- You become what you think about, whether it's hate and evil or love and good.
- Dwell on the good, think of the good, be thankful for the good.
- Put aside your hurts.
- Lawsuits are almost always a waste of your time, money, and energy.
- The only ones who do well in lawsuits are the lawyers.
- How many years do you intend to dedicate to hurting others? How much money could you make in the same time serving others?

- The universe, God, karma—whatever you believe in wants you to be happy and will drive you ahead if hate is not living in your heart and dwelling in your mind.
- Evil is not stronger than good, it is just easier to focus on.
- While you have unlimited opportunity, you don't have unlimited time, so decide what is it you wish to bring into your life and focus your energy there.
- Hate and Resentment are more a reflection of how we view ourselves than anything else.
- Self-pity and jealousy feed into your hate and resentment.
- Be happy for others, speak well of others, forgive others, so good things can come into your life.
- Be grateful for what you have; all accomplishment starts with gratitude.
- Do not speak of your troubles, because what you dwell on comes into your life.
- Speak of things you want in your life, not of things you don't want.
- When others encourage your hatred or jealousy it is to serve their own interest.
- Hatred and jealousy are used to control you, not to help you.
- Avoid negative people in your life lest you catch what they have—and have only what they have.

CHAPTER 7

FORGIVENESS

Anger makes you smaller, while forgiveness forces you to grow beyond what you were.
— *Cherie Carter-Scott*

I had been dreading this conversation for months because I was afraid I knew the answer. I had been kicking myself for not getting the cash up front rather than carrying the note. Every time I had wanted to talk to her Susan was out of the office. I was at a loss as to why I was afraid to speak with her about it. She had promised periodic payments which I had never received, and it had been 13 months with no payment. The original note called for full payment within 12 months. She owed me the money, so since she was never going to bring it up it was up to me. Finally I found her in her office:

"Sue, have you got a minute?"

"Sure, whatcha need?"

"It's been over a year since you promised to pay me the $50,000 for the store. When do you think you can get that to me?"

Sue looked down as if looking for an escape from what was going to be an uncomfortable conversation. "The store isn't making any money. I've been having to put my own money in."

I spoke in a reasonable voice, almost soothing. "Well, I offered to buy it from you a year ago for $50,000, and offered to pay you cash up front. You insisted you wanted the store, and I agreed to give you a year to pay for it. You said you would make payments and I haven't seen a dime yet."

Sue responded indignantly, "That's not what we agreed to."

"Yes it is, Sue," I replied, a bit miffed. Who was she to deny that she owed me the money when we had a written agreement? I could feel a slow burn of anger over the direction this was going. "I have it in writing right here. You agreed to pay me, and I agreed to stay on as an agent paying my normal fees. I have been paying you over two thousand a month—I've paid you half of what you owe me already."

Huffing, Sue replied, "You're just going to have to wait. If the store isn't making any money I am not going to pay you."

I could feel my sense of self-control slipping. I needed that money to keep things afloat for another six months. Without it I was going to be in deep trouble. My voice rose slightly. "That's not what we agreed to. I offered you cash for the business and was decent enough to give you a year to pay me, and now you're telling me you're not going to pay me. What's up with that?"

Dismissively, Sue replied, "You'll simply have to wait, and I will pay you if I can."

It was at this point that I realized she was never going to pay me. I had made a huge mistake in trusting her, and if I wanted my money I was going to have to fight for it. Tersely I said "I've been waiting for over a year for my money and now you're telling me to keep on paying you while you're not paying me Not going to happen."

Sue looked me straight in the eye and said, "Then I guess you will never get your money," with all the coldness she could muster.

You have got to be kidding me. I loan her the money in good faith and here she is screwing me out of it. What a piece of work this woman is. It will be a cold day in hell that I keep working for this brokerage. What was the name of that person at Keller Williams? I know I have it written down somewhere. I am going to call her as soon as I walk out this door and I am going to be out of here tomorrow. If she thinks I won't sue her for that amount of money she is nuts. "Well, we' see about that" I told her. I left her office, calling her a not very flattering name under my breath, disillusioned with my ability to judge people.

Shortly after this episode I left for another brokerage. Under my contract clause I had to pay her a sum approaching $15,000 to depart, even though she had not paid me a cent of what she owed me. Although my staff told me I was insane I made the payment. I determined I was going to do what was right instead of what was easy, and keep my word regardless of whether she kept hers. I also hired an attorney and was successful in getting a judgment against her for $50,000...

Of which I recovered nothing.

For a while I was angry, frustrated and hurt. In a short period of time I accepted that I had done the best I could with what I had known at the time. There was no indication that she would refuse to pay me; we had a contract and she seemed financially stable. The first thing I did is stop beating myself up for losing the money. I adopted the attitude that even if she didn't pay me I would be OK and life would make it up to me down the road. I didn't like who I was when I was focused on the wrong done to me, so I set it aside. Hating her would mean I had to hate myself, and that was a power I was not going to give her.

Later she went through some terrible personal and financial problems of her own. The energy you put out is the energy you get back, and the rebound of her actions was serious indeed. While I will never associate with her again, I don't bear her any animus. You only have so much energy to use in rebuilding your life, growing your business, and realizing your dreams. If you spend that energy in the maintenance of hate, you will have nothing left for love, growth, and the bright future that can be yours.

One of the important things that you have to do in order to move on with your life is to learn how to forgive. The first thing you have to do is forgive yourself. You have to forgive yourself for the mistakes you've made in your personal relationships, and you have to forgive yourself for the mistakes you've made in your business.

There was a time when

I would get up every morning and berate myself for the stupidity of my business decisions, and the things I should have done differently in my personal relationships. However, constantly reinforcing the negative became a self-fulfilling prophecy. Eventually I realized that it was extremely unproductive and destructive to my future. I came to the conclusion that I had done the best I could do with the knowledge I had at the time, and I hadn't intentionally tried to hurt anyone either in my personal or business relationships.

Surprisingly for me, many of the business people with whom I had worked for years were extremely understanding. I owed $5,000 to my

Accountant of twenty years, and I couldn't pay him. When I explained my situation, he pulled out my bill and wrote "Paid in full" on it. He said, "Tom, you've been a great client. You sent me a lot of business over the years. Don't worry about it; we'll do business down the road."

It's very heartwarming when you have that type of relationship. Now, it's a given that not all your business partners will see it the same way. Some will accept that you've done your best and simply let it go as a cost of doing business. Many of those remain your friends. Some will no longer be your vendors or friends but won't pursue you legally, and others will no longer be your business partners or friends and *will* pursue you legally.

It almost goes without saying that many of the financial institutions you've dealt with are going to come after you. You will have to negotiate a settlement with them or make a decision to file bankruptcy and clear the decks so you can start over. Donald Trump was once questioned about going broke. "The world forgives and the world forgets" he said, and I've found that to be extremely true, especially in today's economy. People are understanding. Most people realize that you didn't do anything vindictive, illegal, or malicious. You did your best. You were following the advice of the financial gurus, trying to get ahead, reinvesting your money, and trying to grow your business. That turned and bit you right in the backside.

None of that makes you a bad person. Knowing what you know now, if you could go back and do it differently you would. Since that isn't possible you have to use the knowledge you gained from your failure to move ahead, making sure you don't make the same mistakes twice.

The more difficult problem is forgiving yourself for the mistakes in your personal relationships. In many cases a heartfelt apology and making a sincere effort to do better in the future can repair relationships. In my case, sadly, that wasn't an option. My wife had passed away and I felt a significant responsibility for that. I wondered what I should have done differently, and whether I could have saved her, but the reality of it is that I couldn't have changed the outcome no matter what I did.

After Kathy died I read *The Purpose Driven Life* three times, cover to cover, looking for some meaning in my life. Even though I believed in God, at that point I hated God with all my heart; but I think God understood that and he certainly didn't hate me back. Over time with reflection, thought, prayer and reading I came to the conclusion that there is a plan, I just don't know what that is. When a door closes one opens.

I also realized that Kathy would not want me to be unhappy. She loved me, cared about me and would want me to move on with my life. I know she forgave me for some of the hurtful things that I did, the Lord has forgiven me, and I've forgiven myself for being an imperfect human being.

It took years for the blackness to come out of my heart, for the hate to come out of my soul, for me to start feeling like my old self. So my advice is that if the people you care about in your life are still alive, don't wait—go talk to them. It may be a very uncomfortable conversation and they may not wish to speak with you, but keep trying. Very little in this world is irreversible. How will you feel if that person passes away before you are able to make peace with them? That hurt is more difficult to overcome, so spare yourself if you can. The other thing you have to do is forgive others for the hurts they've done to you. Focusing on the hurts that others inflicted on you does nothing to them. But it does a great deal to you: it drains you mentally, it drains you of your positive attitude, and it drains you of your ability to move forward. Thoughts of revenge, of how to get back at people for what they have done to you, are not productive uses of your time or energy. The universe has ways of getting even with people who treated you poorly. The old saying "What goes around comes around" is more true than people realize. I've known people who have had misfortune, and discovered that people had no sympathy for them. The reason for that is because they never took the time to be good to the people they knew.

Forgiveness doesn't mean you have to be friends with those who have harmed you. You do not need to talk to them or associate with them in any fashion whatsoever. What it does mean is that you have to let go of your anger and hurt so you can focus your energy, thoughts, and personality for more productive pursuits. You need to be about rebuilding your business, social life and relationships. Holding a grudge, being filled with hate towards other people, doesn't hurt them. Rather, it gives them dominion over you. Do you think for one second those people are worried about the fact that you hate them? That you want revenge against them? In your heart, you know the answer is "NO." Not only no, but hell, no. So don't allow all that negative energy to occupy your mind, push out the positive, and poison your future.

The sad reality is that, until you forgive others, they are controlling you. They are keeping you down; they are preventing you from becoming what you want to be. Why would anyone want to give others that power? I've known people that have been involved in lawsuits over amounts as small as $500. The suit drags on for years and cost tens of thousands of dollars, and yet they claim they're standing on principle. I'm not sure what principle that is, except the principle of stupidity in allowing their time, energy, and creative juices to be consumed over something so trifling. Even if it's a larger amount of money or a larger offense against you, at some point you need to let it go if you truly want a life filled with positive energy and experiences.

A useful technique I learned is to step back and get perspective on how you will feel about the matter in six months, a year, or five years. Will you have let it go? You should have. What is your perspective then? If your feelings around the matter have changed then, don't the changed feelings exist even today? Bring those feelings forward to the present, adopt the longer term perspective in the present, and you will be able to set aside the hurts and disappointments rather than dragging them into your future as an anchor on your attitude and abilities.

Once you set that baggage down, it's amazing how much lighter you feel. You can laugh to yourself about how the universe will eventually deal with your enemies. The truth is that the best way to really hurt them is for you to be far better without them than you ever were with them—to do more, be more, and be happy and successful. Hateful people are toxic. They suck the energy out of you. Learn to ignore those people and move on. When you let go of your anger, the self-righteousness and the hate it's like setting down a bag of bricks. You will find your attitude improves, your health improves, your personal relationships improve, and life is better in just about every possible way. Once you forgive yourself and others for slights against you, you're well on your way to be able to rebuild your dreams.

Once you clear the decks of all the business debris and have forgiven yourself for your personal lapses, you need to think about what you really want. Do you want what you used to have, or do you want something different, something more? Do you want to put your life back together in exactly the same fashion it was before or do you want to do it different? You are starting with a clean slate, so your life can be whatever it is you want it to be.

THOUGHTS ON FORGIVENESS

- Forgiveness is a salve on your wounds; it allows you to heal.
- Forgiveness is an act of kindness towards yourself.
- When you forgive others you are helping yourself at the same time.
- It doesn't matter if you're right or wrong; it matters what you want for your future—you may need to be the bigger person.
- Forgiving yourself is critical to your future success.
- Since God has forgiven you the second you asked, don't you think it is time to forgive yourself?
- Being a hater destroys your own future.
- If you can't set down your baggage you are choosing to limit your future.
- There are entire books on forgiveness; perhaps you should read one.
- Whether others forgive you or not, your decision to forgive sets you free of the shackles of negative energy, and your life will be better.

CHAPTER 8

LETTING GO OF THE DISAPPOINTMENT

The only way of catching a train I have ever discovered is to miss the train before.
— *G.K. Chesterton*

Things had been tough for a while. Sales had dropped into the toilet and we were struggling to make payments, but fortunately we were managing to keep up. Selling lots in a dried-up market is very difficult. Not only were we having trouble, but many of the other subdivisions in town were all in the same boat: lots of inventory but no buyers. When we looked at how much we had to get per lot just to break even I didn't see how we were going to make any money on the project in the long term. At this point I was just hoping to get enough out to pay the bank and get our own money back.

In my mind the bank was very lucky to have us. Lots of people had stopped making payments and I was sure they would be happy to renew the loan since we were keeping up with our payments. Every year we had to renew, so it was not surprise when I heard from Marcus.

"Tom, we were hoping you could come into the bank this week. Your note is coming up for renewal and we wanted to talk about renewal terms." I was happy to hear they were talking about renewal. You just never know when it comes to banks.

"Sure Marcus, is tomorrow O.K.?" Since they were talking about renewal I thought I might as well get it out of the way so I could get on to worrying about other things.

Marcus said amicably. "That would work. See you then."

I arrived at 9 a.m., just as the doors were opening. Marcus was already at work, paperwork covering his desk. We began with the small talk bankers always like to use, and then Marcus decided it was time to get down to business.

"Tom, how are things going up at the subdivision?" he inquired.

I told him the truth. He knew the score anyway, and I'd always been upfront with the people I dealt with. "You know Marcus, it's very slow, but we are keeping the bank paid and it will turn around eventually."

Then Marcus dropped the one sentence that spelled the death of our little endeavor. "About that... the FDIC came in and required us to do new appraisals on all of our assets, including the note on your subdivision."

Uh oh, I definitely do not like the sound of that. No sir, not one little bit. When the government gets involved stupidity rules the day—and the night. "Um, ok, what does that mean to me?"

"Well, the appraisal came in at less than a million and the note balance is 1.5 million. In order to renew we are going to need you to bring in $600,000 cash to get it back into the new FDIC regulations." Well, there is that elephant in the room. Didn't figure we would be talking about it. I thought making payments made us immune to such things but alas, it wasn't to be.

I hit Marcus right between the eyes with what I am sure he was expecting. "Marcus, you know I don't have that kind of cash. You guys have raised interest rates 13 times in the last two years. We are making payments, but we don't have that kind of free cash anymore." When the government had decided to slow down the economy they hadn't put out a little of the fire, they put out the whole thing with a fire hose. Fed policy had left us hanging on by the proverbial thread, and here was the FDIC riding in to make sure that thread got snipped.

Marcus told me what intuitively I knew. "Well, if you can't bring it current we will have to foreclose."

I was a little beyond indignant. I had spent years of my life working to build this up and another government policy from the same idiots who had caused the problem was about to ruin my life. "You mean that I have been making my payments for five years and you're going to screw me over. If you take my subdivision you get nothing, nada, zip."

"Well, there is a clause in your loan that says if the loan becomes upside down we can require additional capital contributions."

Clause my ass, where is the common sense in this? When I signed the loan I had asked about this clause and was told it was required but had never been used on people who were making their payments. It looked as if I was going to be the first person they clubbed with this clause. "Marcus, we talked about this when we did the loan. You said you would never use it as long as the payments were being made."

"Well, now the FDIC is requiring us to do it."

Nice to see them passing the buck to higher authority. How about getting some balls and telling them you're not going to kick someone with my payment history to the curb? So much for trusting your banker. "You've got to be kidding me. How does that make any sense? You're going to take a paying loan and turn it into a foreclosure and ruin me in the process. How is that fair?"

I could see Marcus was unhappy having to break the news to me. But, hey, it wasn't his financial future that he had just sealed. "Sorry Tom, it's not my decision at this point. I wish it were different."

I thought I had to state the obvious if only for my own confirmation. "So we are going to lose hundreds of thousands we already invested, plus five years of my life putting this thing together, because the government has its head up its ass."

"I'm afraid so, Tom," Marcus said, with finality of the coffin lid shutting.

The process had just started. I went from my bank to my attorney to see what could be done. My attorney had saved me before, so I was hopeful, but the news wasn't good. He said the bank would ultimately be successful in foreclosing even if I were to fight them. He suggested we give it back with an agreement not to pursue us for additional money or to damage our credit. Although I would lose my money, I would not be liable for anything down the road.

At first the bank balked. However, I told my attorney that if they continued to refuse to work with us that he should ask for a jury trial. I was pretty confident that the bank would have a tough time convincing 12 of my peers that I should lose my subdivision when I had never missed a payment. My attorney said he didn't even know if such a thing was possible, but he passed the word to the bank and they took the property back for what was owed, letting me off the hook.

In retrospect they did me a huge favor. I would have spent the next 10 years struggling to make payments and get the project to breakeven. There was a pretty good chance that I would lose money in the end, as well as a decade or more of my life. I quickly came to the realization that I could earn the money back but I could never get the time back. The peace of mind of not having this project hanging over my head turned into a blessing and has allowed me to recover my finances and my attitude.

Letting go of disappointment was a tough thing for me to learn. After years of struggling to get ahead, to have it all collapse around my ears was heartbreaking. Where did I go wrong? What did I do to deserve this colossal failure?

What I eventually learned was that I needed to look at my disappointment as the seed of something greater. But before I could do that, I had to get a bit philosophical with myself and put my disappointment in perspective. So let's look at what is truly bothering you. Let's drill down to the root so we may more clearly understand what it is that's causing *your* anguish.

When you look at what has happened, what is it truly that bothers you? Is it that your plans did not work out as expected, or is something else lurking in the background? I believe your disappointment stems not from something not working out but rather from what you think your setback is saying about you.

When we are disappointed we often feel it is a reflection on our skill set and abilities. We feel that the disappointment would not have occurred if we were only a little smarter, a little quicker or had a little more ability. This thinking is leading you down a dead end road. You cannot be all-knowing, all-seeing and omnipotent. You will meet with disappointment in your life from time to time.

If your skills need improving, then work to improve them, but do not berate yourself when things don't always work out as planned. Focus on what you want with a positive feeling in your heart and work toward it knowing that you are drawing it into your life.

Often you will feel as if time has been lost and money has been wasted, all for naught. The time spent and the money used in the pursuit of your dream is money spent on your education. You are learning not only about what it is you're trying to accomplish, but also about yourself. You are learning where your skills lie, and what does and doesn't work for your personality. Nothing has been wasted. All can be counted as good if you grow your understanding. Understanding yourself is the first step in achievement. How can you truly know what you are capable of until you actually try?

When you occasionally fail, as all of us do, see it as an opportunity rather than as a setback. Learn the lessons and try again. Necessary, adjust your course. Find a new dream, a new goal, and utilize the knowledge you paid for to do better next time.

Another belief related to your disappointment may be that you let others down. You have not let anyone down; you have simply learned what won't work. If you fail to use what you have learned you may have let others down. But if you're willing to get back up and try again, you have used your disappointment as a motivator for future successes. Everything that happens to you can be a reason to stop trying or a reason to get up and try again. The battle is raging in your mind.

You will almost certainly be disappointed many times. Welcome to the real world. Disappointment does not define your character; it displays it. How do you respond when things don't go as planned? Are you whiny, complaining, and wallowing in self-pity? Or are you tenacious, tough, and willing to learn the lessons attached to the disappointment? Guts and tenacity will carry you far further than any other character traits. Don't let disappointment define you down. Allow it to define you up, to show the character of a champion that is screaming to get out of you.

Disappointment tells you that what you thought you had figured out, you actually had not figured out. That is a blow to your ego as well as your confidence. Many people stop right there and let guilt, shame, and the other deadly life destroyers keep them disappointed till they finally die. They find the blow to their ego too much to bear. They find their confidence compromised and are afraid to trust themselves again.

I have come to believe that mistakes and failure are the universe's way of telling us we are on the wrong path. They are signposts pointing out that somewhere in the past we made a wrong turn. When we see them, they don't mean the trip is over; they simply mean we need to get back on course.

Perhaps you need to backtrack to the time we were successful and begin rebuilding there. Perhaps you can change direction and intersect your path to success. Maybe you landed on the wrong shore and walked in the wrong direction. This is the place where a coach, mentor, honest friend or associate may be able to provide some perspective on your journey. Just be sure the person to whom you turn for advice is on a path you would like to follow.

Your life up to this point is a culmination of your conscious thoughts and the unconscious programs that run much of your life. If you dwell on those things that didn't work out, if you think that "things never work out for me," then guess what? They won't. I hear people all the time speaking disappointment and defeat into their lives. Statements of, "I never seem to get ahead," or "If it wasn't for bad luck I have no luck at all," aren't just statements about your present; they are self-fulfilling prophesies of your future. You must stop prophesying these things into your life. The universe is listening, and when you speak those words it simply assumes further disappointment with your life is what you want and proceeds to deliver it to your door. Until you take control of your own mind and thoughts and begin speaking success into your life, you will continue to be disappointed.

THOUGHTS ON DISAPOINTMENT

- There will be disappointments in your life; get over it.
- Use the disappointments as an indicator that you may be on the wrong path.
- You may be on the wrong path or simply looking the wrong way as you walk your path.
- Use those who have walked your path before successfully to nudge you at your forks in the road.
- Stop talking about your disappointments—no one cares except your subconscious, which will provide more of the same if you keep focusing your thoughts in that area.
- Start speaking success, health and the wonderful things you desire into your life.
- Disappointment doesn't define your character, it displays it.
- Is it the disappointment that is bothering you, or what you believe it says about you?
- What disappointment says about you is totally based on how you react to it.

- Define what is important to you and work toward its accomplishment.
- You can't let anyone down but yourself.
- If you fail to learn from your disappointments you are bound to have something very similar enter your life at another point.
- Learn about yourself, what drives you, and what is important in your mind.
- Give me guts and tenacity over all else; everything else can be learned.

CHAPTER 9

LETTING GO OF THE FEAR OF FAILURE

Successful and unsuccessful people do not vary greatly in their abilities.
They vary in their desires to reach their potential.
— *John C Maxwell*

After Kathy died I moved to a much warmer climate and met an incredible woman, many years my junior. She had the wisdom of someone much older and was a wonderful sounding board. We met at the condo where I lived shortly after my arrival, and we quickly became inseparable. Jo helped me through some of my issues around my wife and her death, and also taught me how to live cheaply. She made an incredible living as an international model but had a goal of retiring by 30, since the working life of a model is limited. In order to do so she lived modestly and taught me what was really important: the people in our lives, rather than the material baggage we seem to accumulate.

Jo was instrumental in getting me back on an even keel and beginning to revive my true entrepreneurial spirit. She was never afraid to say what she thought—something I dearly love about her. While sitting at home one evening a typical topic came up. . .

"Tom, why don't you go out on your own again? You don't need that other guy." Jo had been urging me to consider going out on my own again for some time. She often told me that she didn't trust the person I was working with, and I should be careful about him.

I thought about what I wanted to say. "Jo, I'm not sure I can generate leads. At least now I am making enough to get by." Even while saying it I knew I was wrong. I had been generating all my own leads for almost a year.

"And he is keeping most of the money with you doing all the work." Jo really knew where to hit me—in the pocketbook. Of course she was right. She knew what I was making and how much I was working to make it.

"Yeah, but I don't know the market that well. What if I can't make a living?" I was afraid to try again. My upbringing and society seemed to reinforce that when we fail we need to feel sad and be afraid to try again.

Jo, who had been on her own since she was 16, wasn't having any of that. "You know you can make a living. You always have. You are the one doing the work. Don't you think you should get paid for it?"

She was putting a fine point on what I already knew. "I know I'm getting shafted, but frankly I can't take the risk."

Sometimes you need someone who knows you well to tell you the truth, and this evening Jo was going to make sure I knew what the truth was. "What risk? You're already taking all the risk for half the money. Don't you think he'd kick you to the curb in a second if he thought he could make more money?" Her insight was to prove incredibly accurate in just a few more months.

"Without a doubt, but after getting my butt kicked I'm more worried about getting killed again."

I knew I was cowering under my bed like a little girl, but failure in business is like touching a hot stove; you don't want to do it again.

"You're worrying too much. You can always make enough to get by if worse comes to worse. Look at what happened before; they basically took everything you had and you got by."

She was right, of course. I had taken the worst the world could throw at me, both personally and financially, and I was still standing. Well, maybe crawling—but I was moving.

"And I don't want that to happen again." I knew I was on the losing end of this argument.

Jo saw I was weakening in my whining and moved in for the kill. "Well sitting on your butt waiting for something to happen isn't going to help."

Nice to see she wasn't going to be subtle about it. Nothing like a kick to the groin. "I know, but I'm a bit gun shy. What if things go down the tubes again?"

"When I met you, you had nothing. Do you think that matters to me? When you're at the bottom there is only one way to go; otherwise you stay broke forever."

Why doesn't she just tell me to get some balls? Well, she was obviously right. I had been moping long enough. Time to get up off the floor, throw off the covers of self-doubt and move on. And that's just what I did. Shortly thereafter Jo's schedule took her out of town. Since the only thing really holding me had left I elected to do the same and decamped back to where I came from with a determination to rebuild. Her belief in me helped me to gather the courage to face my fears, knowing that no matter what came against me I would prosper.

When things don't go as you plan there is always a fear that if you try again, something may go wrong again. The embarrassment many people feel is often reinforced by unsupportive friends and family as well as by society. Sadly, it is true that some people you know may feel better about themselves if you fail. They can then reinforce their own beliefs that attempting to do something different, to get out of their job, build a business, or attempt something great is simply beyond the reach of people who aren't born rich or special.

The old saying, "Failure isn't Fatal," bears remembering. It's also very important to notice that those who look down on you for failure are almost never those who have made it to the top in any field of endeavor. Those who have made it understand the role that failure plays in success. If you don't fail you will not succeed. Failure is the training ground for high performance. Show me someone who hasn't failed and I will show you someone who hasn't tried.

So why are you listening to people who are like children, cowering in the dark, afraid of their own shadows? Many are trading their lives working for someone else, accepting scraps off the table of life when they could pull up chair if they only had the courage to try.

The masses convince themselves that their life goal should be to get a secure job with benefits, work 40 years for someone else, and then retire "comfortably." While that may have worked for your parents' generation, it is no longer true. Having a job is the riskiest thing you can do. Most companies will fire you in a heartbeat if it will put a few extra bucks on the bottom line. The days when you could trade your loyalty to the company in exchange for the company's loyalty to you are long gone, and won't be coming back in our lifetime. Your only security lies in what you know and what you can do for others.

Those who are afraid to fail are destined to fail. You can't win the game of life by playing defense. You need to go on offense—attack life, shake it until it gives you exactly what you demand. Those who are willing to step up will fail from time to time. Frankly, there is no guarantee that you will make it the next time you try, but you need to decide how you want to live your life. Do you want to stand at the plate and keep swinging the bat until you learn how to connect, or do you want to call yourself out? You are the only one who can call you out. No other person, and certainly not society, has the power to do that.

My personal belief: "Failure isn't fatal, but failure to try is the slowest and most painful way to die." To paraphrase an ancient writer, those courageous enough to try may die once, but those without courage are destined to die many times in their heart and soul.

Keep failure in perspective. If failing in your particular field of endeavor isn't fatal, than what is holding you back? Embarrassment about what people may say? To put it bluntly, screw them. They don't pay your bills. If you succeed, they will be the first to say you had it easy or somehow lucked into it. They are generally gutless cowards. Use negative people as a negative reinforcement to push yourself ahead. Think how much you will enjoy driving past them in your new car (slowly, to let them take a good look) or having a newspaper or magazine article written about you extolling your great success, while they still wallow in their mediocrity.

When you begin to laugh about your failures and tell funny stories about them, you are developing the right attitude and letting go of your fear. It may be less than funny when you're going through it, but as you gain distance and time from the actual event your perspective begins to change. The great thing is: you get to choose your perspective.

When things are bad I try to put myself in my shoes a couple of years down the road. I mentally picture myself successful and happy, looking back on my current place and time. Looking at the situation from different angles, I try to find the good in where I am right now. And as bad as each situation may be, there is always a kernel of good to be found.

If you're living in a basement as I was at least you don't have much to clean and you're living cheap, which will help you to start rebuilding. That's a kernel of good. If you have lost your job you now have the opportunity to do what you always have wanted to try—a kernel of good. If your spouse has left you, you have an opportunity to upgrade—a kernel of good. Those situations pale in comparison to the loss of a loved one, so they are easier to deal with. But even if you have lost a loved one you have been blessed to have them in your life. And while they were taken prematurely, would you really rather have never known them? There is your kernel of good, in the great fortune you had to be privileged to know someone truly special.

Ask yourself when you are looking back from your future self: what lessons did I learn, how do I feel about it now, what paths were shown to me that would not otherwise have revealed themselves? How will you feel at that point in the future? If you can feel that way in the future, why not pull that feeling forward into the present and focus on feeling that way today? You will be known as an unshakable person when you develop the habit of future perspective today. Others will think you wise, charismatic, thoughtful, and a worthy role model.

The way you will feel in the future lives within you today. Take the time to bring it forth into your present and the light will once again shine in your life. Your fear of failure will diminish with time, and by using future perspective you set the clock forward in your mind and jump start your road to recovery.

THOUGHTS ON FAILURE

- If you haven't failed you haven't tried.
- Adults act, children cower—so get some guts.
- Stop worrying about failing; that's how you learn.
- Those who give you grief over your failure haven't the courage to try themselves—so what are you still doing listening to those people, anyway?
- The same people who give you grief for failure will say you had it easy when you succeed, so pitch them over the side (figuratively, of course).
- I can live with the failure, but I can't live with not trying.
- Courage isn't an absence of fear; it is recognizing the fear and doing it anyway.
- Inside every negative event or failure is a kernel of good, waiting to blossom.
- Perspective is developed over time. Since perspective takes time, shorten the process by focusing on your future self and your future perspective on the current events. Bring that feeling into the present and allow it to alter your feelings today.
- Tomorrow's perspective is available today; adopt it, use it.
- Those with perspective are looked upon with admiration.
- Nothing is worse than the loss of a loved one, but never forget your true blessing in knowing them.

- When you learn to laugh about your failures, you are truly on the road to recovery.

CHAPTER 10

LETTING GO OF THE FEAR OF SUCCESS

Winning isn't everything, but wanting to win is.
— Vince Lombardi

"Thanks for the offer, Tom, but I'm happy as an instructor." Our Supervising Instructor had left the company for another job and I was offering that position, and more money, to Leah. This was not going as I had planned. Why would she turn down a promotion? I'd thought for sure she would be excited and jump at the opportunity.

"So you're saying you don't want the job?" It was one of those days where I felt the need to state the obvious.

Leah bit her lip and looked down slightly. *Ah ha!* I thought. *Something else is bothering her.* "Leah, what's the real reason you aren't interested in this promotion? Is it the money?" Experience had taught me that when people hesitate it is almost always about the money.

"No, the money is fine,"

Well, so much for that theory. She should have said yes and worked me for more money when I gave her the opening. She certainly could have gotten me to offer a few grand more even if it wasn't about the money.

"Would you mind sharing what is really bothering you?" I asked in a fatherly tone. In my late 30s I was the old man of the place.

"It's nothing. I just saw how Mary lost friends when she took the job."

Now we were getting somewhere. Mary's management style was a little brusque, something I had been working on with limited success. I was actually contemplating demoting her when she made the decision to leave and saved me the trouble.

"Leah, what is it you think caused Mary's conflicts with the instructors?" I was thinking Leah was a much different person, and I wanted her to see she was not Mary.

"I'm not sure, but I don't want to take the job and have everyone hating me." Leah was sharp, but maybe she was a little too soft for this job. On the other hand, perhaps this was what we needed—someone who was empathetic and used consensus and a soft touch. After all, the instructor personalities were easily offended by a heavy hand.

"Do you think I want you to run things exactly the way Mary did?"

"Ahhhh, I don't know. . ." She was starting to see the light.

"Leah, being the boss, getting promoted, being successful is not about stepping on people; it's about building people up. Everything you want you have to get through your relationships with other people. Most people are afraid if they get promoted their friends won't like them, they will have to be hard on people—in other words, they have to be like the person they are replacing." Sorry, Mary, but I wasn't telling Leah anything she didn't already know.

"Leah, I am offering you this job because I see something in you, something great. Now, are there going to be times you have to do things you don't want to do. Of course there are going to be those times. What I think I hear you saying is that you wouldn't want to do things the way Mary did them. What I did as I got promoted is look at what my boss did, and their boss. I took what I liked and pitched the rest. You have to make the job your own, with your own style. You have to get the job done, but it doesn't need to be done the way it has been in the past."

Leah was brightening up. "You mean I can run things the way I want?"

"Within reason," I told her. "You need to make sure the classes are covered and the instructors are doing their jobs, but other than that, as long as the instructors are happy and things are going smoothly I stay out of your hair."

There was that room-melting smile everyone loved. "I'm not saying you're not going to possibly lose friends. Often when you're the boss people won't be as close to you. But what you need to think about is your future. You've only been out of college two years. Will these be the friends you have the rest of your life? Maybe, but more than likely not."

I paused to see if I was getting through. Leah was nodding. "You need to ask yourself if true friends would be happy for you or try to make your life difficult and hold you back. No matter where you go, there are going to be people who are in your corner and happy about your success, and those that will be jealous and not at all supportive. Keep the ones who are in your corner close and ignore the others. Your success does not hurt others. You can't help them by holding back and hoping you won't offend anyone. If you do, you will never make any serious money or get ahead in anything."

Leah's mind was whirling; I could see it in the distant stare on her face. Was she running her future in her own mind, contemplating how to politely decline, or seriously considering what I said?

Leah's head snapped up. "About the money. . ." *Note to self, stop asking if it is about the money. This is going to cost me some.*

Leah went on to become a great manager and team leader. Her style was warm yet her expectations were clear. We lost touch after I sold the company, but a couple of years later she contacted me to let me know she was in charge of a much bigger operation and to thank me for what I had done for her. Leah, wherever you are—you go girl!

When you look at people who almost grasped the brass ring and then failed, you sometimes ask yourself why they didn't make it. I believe most people have a fear of failure—and many people have a fear of success. Usually it is not conscious; rather, it is a subconscious belief of not being worthy of success. People with that feeling manage to manifest that failure in their life. Until you truly believe you are worthy of success, failure will haunt you.

People often have beliefs about money, success and their own self-worth that are baggage from earlier years. Unconsciously they may be uncomfortable making more money than their parents made. They may believe their friends won't like them if they become wealthy. Or—the ideas that are especially difficult to root out—statements from parents, teachers, religious leaders, and others that got down in their subconscious when they were young, just waiting to stab them in the back when they least expect it. That was true for me.

Many of us with religious upbringings have been indoctrinated with the belief that money is the root of all evil. What the Bible actually says is, "the love of money is the root of all evil." Money is neither good nor evil; it has only the meaning we give it. If your pursuit of money is the sole focus of your life, then money has become your God. Yourself-worth will be tied up in what you own and in appearing to have more than those around you. You will most likely never achieve great success, since your attitude about money is about appearances. You feel that your possessions will give you the joy and happiness that is missing from your life, and they may do that temporarily, but in no time you will be looking for a bigger car, a bigger home, a prettier or more handsome significant other. What you have will never be enough, and the universe will hold you back until your attitude matures.

On the other hand, if you understand money for what it is, and you know what it can and can't do for you, you stand a much greater chance of having it. Let there be no doubt in your mind: I am in favor of lots of money. While money may not buy happiness, it buys you the luxury of focusing your efforts on non-monetary concerns. When you argue with your husband or your wife, it often is either directly or indirectly about money. When you and your spouse are arguing about what kind of car to buy, or where to send the kids to school, it's about more than the car or school. Oftentimes it is about the car you would really like but can't afford, or what school you would like to send the kids to that is out of your financial reach.

So by all means, make lots of money, but remember money can buy you things you will shortly be tired of, or experiences and memories that will be with you forever. Stop and think for a moment about the wonderful times in your life. Were they about the cars, boats, motorcycles or planes? Or were they about the people you surrounded yourself with and the experiences you had? It is almost always the experiences, the friends, and the family that come to mind. While some argue that it was their things that allowed them to have those experiences, those things were simply a facilitation of the experience, not the experience itself.

There are many good courses on how to release these negative feelings of self-worth that are unconsciously holding you back. The one I used was called *The Missing Secret* by Dr. Joe Vitale. Joe will walk you through your attitudes about self-worth, money, relationships, and many other areas of your life in which you are not achieving your dreams and I highly recommend this course. You can find a link to Joe's life-changing training at my website, www.YouAreTough.com.

THOUGHTS ON FEAR OF SUCCESS

- Wanting it is not enough; you have to truly believe you deserve it.
- Money doesn't buy you happiness, it buys you options.
- Money buys you freedom and the time to explore your life and your world.
- The accumulation of possessions is a short-term fix for a long-term problem in your life.
- Stuff will make you happy for a short period, but then it becomes a burden.
- Happiness comes through relationships.
- Close friends and family make life a joy.
- Those who truly love you believe in you and think you are worthy of success.
- The universe is simply waiting for you to ask and believe so it can begin delivering.

- Teaching others to be successful opens the doors to your own success.
- Give of your time and knowledge to others who desire it; this builds your worthiness quotient.

CHAPTER 11

LIFESTYLE REDESIGN

Selfishness is not living as one wishes to live, it is asking others to live as one wishes to live.
— *Oscar Wilde*

"George, I am really not sure what I want to do."

George has been a friend of mine since the mid-90s when we both worked for the same car company. George and his wife Cheryl have been there for me through good and bad, offering everything from a place to stay to a job and a perspective that I value. This evening they had invited me down for one of their great steak dinners. Dinner, drinks, and breakfast the next morning always seem to work their magic. Tonight I was thinking out loud.

George had done very well in the car business, rising to the top position of a large company. "Well, you could always go back into the car business. We always have a spot for you, and you would make great money again." The offer had always been open, not only from George but from others with whom I had worked and who now were in a position of authority. It was truly heartwarming to have people offer to save me from financial ruin, even if I decided not to take them up on it.

I had thought extensively about taking George up on his offer. But I was afraid it would kill my dreams. My faith in myself and my desire to achieve might have faded from a roaring fire to a small, flickering candle, but I could feel it growing in strength month after month. I wanted to give it another try. "Yeah, I appreciate that. But I'm afraid if I go back to a regular job I'll never leave, and that scares me more than anything."

"Well, what is it you want to do?" George's voice sounded reasonable, but I could sense that he thought I was nuts not to take him up on the offer.

I thought for a moment about what I had before. I had learned what I didn't want, but what did I want? "I don't know, but I certainly don't want to be so important in the day-to-day business anymore. Did that, got the tee shirt and didn't like it. Never any time off, married to the damn job."

Everyone knew I was a real estate guy. They had seen the beautiful home and lifestyle real estate had given me—and they had seen what it had taken away. It wasn't a very big leap for George to make the connection. "Are you going back into real estate?"

"Probably, at least for now," I responded, almost resigned. "I want to make sure that the business can run without me. I want to get a couple hundred units bought up so that I have passive income coming in and I don't have to worry about where my next paycheck is coming from."

George listened; he is great at listening. I continued, making my own counterargument. "With real estate you're unemployed every morning, and I've seen too many older realtors who are still selling real estate, not because they want to but because they have to."

"Passive income is the way to go or you'll never be able to quit busting your hump," he agreed. George knew the score, knew that if people don't take care of themselves they are going to be retiring miserable. He and Cheryl were going to be fine. They have brains and common sense, which is not so common anymore.

I was glad to hear he didn't think I had gone totally flaky. "I hear that. Going to work every day for someone else's dream is not for me. I would rather die broke having tried than have accepted a paycheck my entire life."

"Hey now, a few of us still have jobs," he protested.

Oops, I didn't mean that the way it came out. But George knew I am not one to judge. "You know what I am talking about. There is nothing wrong with a job. It just won't create the lifestyle I want. I want to be able to work two months and take a month off, disappear for the winter to a beautiful island and come back to more money in the bank than when I left—you know, freedom" Cheryl seemed to love that idea and chimed in, giving George grief about the hours he puts in.

"It would be nice. I'm sure most people wish they could do that." George is the kind of boss most people would love to have, 100% behind his people and his friends.

We had had this conversation before. We both realize most people don't excel because they are more afraid of losing what they have than willing to take a risk that has only a chance of gaining something better. "They could, but most people are too afraid to take the chance. They have houses, cars, kids, and they figure they're stuck with the responsibilities. I think those things are reasons to do something, but most people use it as a reason to sit tight."

"Most people aren't as crazy as you," he smiled. Well, wasn't that the pot calling the kettle black? You don't rise to the top of any organization without being a little daft, and George was the top dog in his business.

"You think? Most people don't think outside the box, that's for sure." Most are willing to accept what comes their way. Some of us are willing to put it all on the line to do something great. "Give me a couple of years and I'll be back on top. But I'm definitely going to do it with a different mindset this time. I used to want to be important; kind of turned me on. Now I just want the check and the time off to pursue what really interests me. It'll be nice to wake up again not worrying about what's in the checkbook."

"If anyone can do it, you can."

Gotta love those who love and support you. Perhaps another cocktail and we can solve the rest of the world's problems. "Thanks George, I appreciate you being there for me."

As you set your mental baggage down and get ready to reenter the fight, it pays not to jump too quickly. This is your opportunity to make new decisions, to determine what it is you want to be in the future. As we ask our children, "What do you want to be when you grow up?" Now is your time to make that decision anew. Your setback is simply a setup for a greater future. It may not have been fair, but it is part of your destiny. That chapter of your life is closed, and it's time to turn the page.

Our parents had far fewer opportunities available to them. They married young, had children young, and expected 40-plus hours a week of soul-crushing work, with the hope of a small pension, retirement and social security to support them in a style that would be at least halfway comfortable for them. That is not your divine destiny. You are destined for greater things simply by reason of the fact that you are searching for something better for your life.

Nonetheless, the path for us is sometimes not clear. There are far more options and far more opportunities, creating new issues for us to deal with. Even if we wanted a pension and social security like our parents had, the social contract between individuals and businesses is no longer there, and government will never be able to support you in any style other than basic subsistence. The thought of accepting more years of spirit-sucking work for a small pittance that won't allow you to travel or do the things you want to do should be more frightening to you than taking the risk to rebuild your life in harmony with your biggest dreams. Ending your days scratching out a living after a lifetime of work is a very sad end to what can be a glorious life for you and your loved ones. It's not a fate you need to accept.

Some of us have never truly admitted what it is we want for ourselves and our lives. We have buried our desires, our hopes and our dreams so deeply that we cannot even be honest with ourselves. When we were children, did we have problems dreaming? No, we dreamed about going to interesting places and doing all kinds of interesting, world-changing things. Why then do we have problems doing so as adults? I believe it is because our dreams were encouraged as harmless fantasies when we were young, but as we matured those around us convinced us that we needed to be realistic and practical, and stop dreaming about things that are never going to happen.

It's time to get back to your dreams.

Sit in silence on a regular basis and let your mind wonder. Start looking back at the dreams you used to have, and imagine a future where those dreams have come true. It's alright; it is healthy to let yourself dream. Your dreams will become the impetus of the actions you take to create a better life for you and those you love. If you're concerned about what people will say, keep your dreams to yourself for now. Build a perfect place in your mind, a place where all things are possible. Whether you spend time in silence sitting in your car, on your deck, or in your favorite chair, let the dreams start. At first, you will probably find that your dreams are like a tiny bubbling brook, filled with small dreams that you consciously believe are possible—dreams of being able to pay your bills, buy a home, pay for a nice car or vacation. Over time your stream will grow, and bigger dreams will be released into your mind. Soon you will have a raging river full of life and dreams for the future. This is the place where lifestyle redesign begins to grow, where you become who you truly want to be.

Like many of you, when I was building my business I built it in such a way that I was the most important cog in the wheel. I wasn't building a business, I was building a job. I was no different than a doctor, lawyer or accountant. I had to be there in the performance loop to make my income. If you are critical to your business—if your income stops whenever you take a break—you've built yourself a job. If that's really your dream, go ahead and rebuild your life in the same fashion. But if you want something different you're going to need to think differently. Only you can decide what you want to be, and what you want to do with the time you have left.

Once you've determined what you want, you must begin with the end in mind. You can rebuild your business and your life in a manner that will allow you to reach your goals. When I started out as an entrepreneur my goal was simply to grow. I didn't have much of a plan, as I suspect most entrepreneurs don't. You wake up one morning and you're tired of what you do, you hate going to work, and you realize you've worked yourself into a corner. Now is the opportunity to change that. When I looked at my business I determined I was critical to the business; I was the limiting factor. When you have become critical to the success of your business you will find yourself working far more than you wish and your business growth will stagnate. You will be stuck, unhappy, overworked, wondering how you are going to ever put down the reins of what you have created.

There are only so many days you can work and if you are the important part of the business, then you are the limiting factor. I determined that I didn't want to be that important. There were other things I wanted to do with my life besides just work. I realized that my failure had given me the opportunity I needed to step aside and rebuild my business so that that the business provided me with an income, but not the stress. I needed to separate what I wanted to be, and what I was, from how I made my money. For years I was what I did, and I wanted that merry-go-round ride to end.

Lifestyle design is not about showing up 40 hours or more each week for the same job, year after year, except for two weeks of vacation per year, and hoping for a small raise every other year. Lifestyle design is about determining what you want and finding a financial vehicle to get you there. If you want to work 60 hours a week and build a business, by all means, be my guest. I think many people find as you get older that the things you sacrificed in order to build that type of business are the things they regret the most: their friends, family and relationships.

What I am about to tell you is one of the most critical things you need to wrap your mind around. When you look back on your life do you think about the things you own, or about the people you spent time with, the activities you were involved with, and the adventures you experienced? As for me, I think about my friends and family, and the things I've done, the places I've been, and the laughs I've had with them. All the material items were nothing but excess baggage—baggage that cost me money, baggage that required monthly payments, insurance, cleaning, and a place to store. I'm not a big believer in living in poverty or minimalism, but I have come to the conclusion that for me life experiences are far more important than accumulating a bigger house, another car or a bigger boat.

Lifestyle design allows you to make time for what you believe is important. If people look at you strangely when you tell them about your dreams and how you're rebuilding your life, you might be on the right track. Part of lifestyle design is making sure you understand what money is and what money isn't and putting money in its proper prospective. I've been rich and I've been broke, and I like being rich better—not because of the things I could buy, but because of the peace of mind it offered. For years I thought I needed five to ten million dollars in the bank so that I could retire, travel the world, live comfortably and not worry about money. What I came to understand was that it wasn't the money I wanted; it was the lifestyle I believed that money could buy me. When I actually calculated what I really needed to provide that kind of lifestyle, I found it was far less than I had thought.

If you have a million dollars in the bank and you earn 5% on that money, that's slightly more than $4,000 per month. Accumulating a million dollars in cash is fairly difficult for most people, but building a business that provides you with $4,000 a month in income is far more understandable and far easier to reach. That same million dollars could earn you $8,000 per month if it were more aggressively invested. So what money is for me is piece of mind. It means that when you wake up in the morning you know you have money coming in that month and every month, you have money in the checking account, and you don't have to worry about paying for food, the power bill or the mortgage. You don't have to worry if the car breaks down because you have money in the bank to cover that expense. Money comes in regularly, providing for the lifestyle you desire.

Money isn't an end-all, and money doesn't love you back. At one point I was living in a 6 bedroom, 4 bath, 5,000-square-foot house on the lake with a boat, cars and a hot tub. It was one of the saddest times of my life. I thought by having those things I would have more friends, my family and friends would be hanging out at my house, and life would be one party after another, but that wasn't what happened. I was so busy trying to maintain and pay for what I had that I didn't have time for my friends, and consequently they didn't have time for me. I learned that money can buy security and peace of mind, but it can't buy happiness. When you stand over the grave of a loved one and think about all the money you made together, it means nothing. Your money won't keep you warm at night and you can't take it with you.

So although money is important, you shouldn't make money your focus when rebuilding. Focus on the lifestyle, the things you want to do, the things you want to have, the places you want to go, and the people you want to meet. Design your income-generating activities around that vision. When you take a close, unemotional look at your balance sheet you might find that you are in a better financial position than you think you are. You might find that your financial resources are enough to support the lifestyle you want or the lifestyle you want to rebuild in a very short time period. The vehicle I chose is real estate; it's the business I've been in and it's the business I understand. My analysis showed that in order to have a $10,000 per month income I need to have fifty units that each clear a $200 per month after all expenses are paid. When I broke it down into smaller pieces, that became a very reasonable goal.

THOUGHTS ON LIFESTYLE

- Lifestyle is about dreams—the ones you used to have plus your new ones.
- It is hard to think about dreams when your checkbook is empty, but it is a necessary step in your financial recovery.
- Lifestyle is a personal choice.
- Don't let others tell you what you should want; decide for yourself what it is you want.
- Dreams need to stretch you, but a dream is just a wish unless you put effort behind it.
- If you think your government is going to take care of you, you're in for a serious disappointment.
- If you think your company is going to take care of you, you're in for a serious disappointment.
- Your only security comes from what occupies the space between your ears.
- You have far more opportunities than earlier generations, but that also means you have far more choices.
- A business is just a high-pressure job if it depends on you.
- Self-employment is not necessarily a business.
- Determine your dreams, what it is you want, and build your business around that lifestyle choice.
- Lifestyle is about more than the things you own, it is about experiences and the people with whom you share them.

- Cash flow is the name of the game; generate cash flow and financial problems vanish.
- If you break down what you need to do to generate the lifestyle you want into smaller pieces, each piece will be doable; if you still think the steps are too big you haven't broken them down into small enough pieces.
- Your future success is going to be at the four-way intersection where your talents, dreams, ambition, and action meet.

CHAPTER 12

MENTORS

No great thing was ever accomplished without a team.
– Loral Langemeier

Thor slid a check in front of me. "I need a second signature on this check." Company policy was that two managers had to sign on any check over $500.

"No problem." I glanced at the check and my eyes bulged. 2.2 million dollars! I had never seen a check that large before, much less signed one. My hand hesitated and I glanced up to see Thor with a smile on his face. "Um. . . What is this for?" I asked. Was a Cayman Island bank account in Thor's future?

"FIFO adjustment for the end of the tax year." FIFO, for the non-accountants in the audience, stands for "First In, First Out." It was the accounting method used by the auto dealership for—well, for something.

I commented wryly, "I hope I'm not liable for this. If I am, I'm going to be a little short." Thor laughed, picked up the check and left.

Thor and I had worked together for years. He had originally hired me at another auto dealership, and when he was promoted to General Manager, he asked me to come along as his Sales Manager. Of course he neglected to mention that they had gone through three Sales Managers in the last 12 months.

When I first met Thor, he was the Sales Manager for a Saturn Auto Store. Saturn was the hot brand at the time, and sales person turnover was almost nonexistent. I had heard how much the sales people were making and I was determined to get a position with the store.

When I applied he informed me that no positions were available. I told him, "You might as well hire me, because I am going to keep showing up and bothering you until you do." Thor laughed at my audacity and invited me to keep in touch.

Thirty days later, on the same day of the month, at the same time of the day, I showed up on his office doorstep. "Never thought I would see you again," Thor said. He mentioned that many spoke of their willingness to keep trying but few followed through. He invited me into his office where he took the time to learn more about me, and what I wanted. He thanked me for keeping in touch. I told him, "You might as well hire me, because I am going to come in every month until you do, or get a restraining order." He laughed again.

Another month passed, and I showed up again. And thirty days after that; month after month I returned, always on the same day and always at the same time. Thor began to expect me, and would have the coffee ready. Soon we were spending an hour or more each month discussing the car business. Without knowing it, Thor began grooming me, mentoring me into an incredible sales person, and later his Sales Manager.

Your mentor may not only guide you; if they believe in your ability they may even elevate you. But first you have to find the right mentor and convince them that coaching you isn't going to be a waste of their time.

Who do you turn to for advice? Have they accomplished what it is you're trying to do? Are you sure? If the person you are looking to for advice hasn't accomplished the thing you want to accomplish, do not listen to them. Find someone who has done what you want to do, or something very similar, and follow in their footsteps.

There are plenty of people who hold themselves out as experts who are not. There are probably people in your life who have opinions about what you should or shouldn't do. Why are you letting them influence you? Are they on the success path or just blending in? If you are going to be successful you need to hang out with and model the people that you want to be like.

If possible recruit your role model as a mentor, either by using your charm or, if necessary, by buying your way in. "Whatever it takes" needs to become your motto. When you choose a mentor or partner, do so up, not laterally. What I mean by that is, choose mentors or partners who have done what you want to do, not others at your level who have not accomplished what you seek for yourself. The only reason to consider a partner at your level is if they complement your skills and bring something critical to the success of the endeavor—but that's a partnership, not a mentor relationship.

You want mentors who are the leaders in their field. A list of mentors to possibly consider is available under the resource tab on my website, www.YouAreTough.com.

The role of a mentor is varied. It will change depending on where you are in your business and even where you are in your personal development and growth. But it's important to understand first what a mentor is *not*. Your mentor is not your friend. That does not mean you can't have a friendly relationship with them, but their purpose in your life is not to be your buddy.

You work with a mentor because you don't know what you don't know. A mentor's primary mission is open your mind to the possibilities of your life and to hold you accountable for your actions. Your mentor has done what you want to do, learning lessons along the way that they will impart to you.

If you've chosen wisely, you have a mentor who has accomplished what you're trying to accomplish, and probably made many mistakes in the achievement of their goals. With that experience, they can show you how to avoid the same mistakes and pitfalls, shortening your road to success. But they are only guides, not magicians. Whether your path to your success will actually be shorter or not depends on how willing you are to listen to what your mentor tells you and implement it in your business and life.

People will often ask my advice on real estate matters and then argue with me about my answer. I often laugh and ask them why they bothered to ask if they weren't interested in my answer. If you're unwilling to listen to the advice of your mentor, then either you need a new mentor or you're simply not ready for the success you say you want.

The best way to prepare yourself to get the most value from your work with a mentor is to know what you want your life to look like down the road, whether that be one year, five years, or an even longer time frame. Your mentor can help outline the steps necessary to complete your goal when the goal is clear. Once the steps have been outlined, a mentor can be extremely useful in guiding you through each of the steps in turn. While all of us would like the end to be achieved quickly, success is almost always a matter of taking it one step at a time.

Your mentor can help keep you from wandering off the path into irrelevant matters. When you're growing a business there are always steps that are critical to your success, and other steps that are nice but not critical. You need to focus on the steps that are critical for you to personally accomplish. Many matters that need to be done do not need to be done by you, and your mentor can tell you which tasks are critical for your own focus and involvement. Noncritical tasks can be delegated with minimal risk and expense, and free up your personal time for better use.

The primary role of your mentor is to open your mind to the possibilities, to new ways of thinking, to expand your understanding of what is possible and how to accomplish whatever you have set your mind on accomplishing. The secondary goal of a mentor is to hold you accountable.

The reason a mentor should not be a good friend is because there are going to be times when you need a serious kick to the backside. If you are not listening to your mentor's advice, if you are not accomplishing what you committed to accomplish, a true mentor is going to let you have it right between the eyes. Good mentors are not afraid to tell you directly what you're doing wrong and what you need to change. If you are sensitive or prone to argue when people criticize you, then you need to set those feelings and attitudes aside and remember why you asked for help in the first place. You needed help because you didn't know everything already.

Many people take personal offense when challenged or held to account for poor performance. If you are one of those people, and want a successful mentoring experience, my advice to you is simple: get over it. I find that when I take offense I am invariably at fault. If you are unable to convince your mentor that you are correct in a matter, then you are almost certainly wrong. Your mentor is your teacher, parent, and priest, all rolled up into one. Your mentor is doing you a favor by working with you and you need to respect what they are saying even more when it is difficult to hear. It's just like sports: the tougher and more demanding the coach, the higher the performance of the athlete. Do you want to be a world-class performer, or don't you?

I've had my own uncomfortable "Come to Jesus" conversations with mentors. I still remember an early wake-up call my real estate coach gave me when he checked in to see what I had accomplished of the goals I had set. My coach and his team had sold over 400 homes in the last year and I had hired him to help me get started.

"So how have things gone the last month?" he asked.

I was prepared for this question. "Great! I got the advertising set up, the office organized and ready to go and the phone lines up and running. I also read the books you suggested on the last call and did a couple of open houses and—" My coach cut me off.

"How many houses did you sell?"

"Um, none—but I have been busy." It sounded lame even as I said it.

"And how much money did you make?"

Ouch. He'd nailed me with just two short questions.

"None, but—" My coach cut me off. He had heard all the excuses in the book before, and didn't need to hear mine.

"Well, how many people did you get as clients, how many buyers, and how many listings?"

I hesitated. "I spoke to a bunch of people at the open houses but I didn't list any homes." I felt like a school boy being chastised for not doing his homework.

"So have you followed up with those people you met at the open houses?" my coach asked.

"Well, no, they didn't want to give me their information." The picture was becoming clear even to me.

My coach persisted. "How many people are you talking to each day?"

I certainly didn't want to answer that question. "Well, maybe one or two." More like one, but I was trying to retain at least a little credibility.

My coach sighed on the other side of the phone. "So basically you did nothing, at least nothing that produces revenue. Am I just wasting my time with you?" I was beginning to wonder myself at this point.

My coach continued. "Tom, I am happy to work with you, but you won't be in business long if you don't talk to people and turn them into clients." A long uncomfortable silence spread across the line. "When you're ready to listen and do what I say let me know and call me back, but until then I think we are just wasting our time here."

This was not at all how I expected this call to go. "No, don't give up on me yet," I pleaded. "I know I can do it."

Another long pause on the phone.

"Are you finally willing to do what I say, what is necessary to make money in this business?"

He hit me right between the eyes with that one. Was I ready to finally do the difficult work to make it in real estate?

"Tell me what I need to do and I will do it." I couldn't fail; there was no fallback position for me. I would either stand and fight and win where I was or I would go down swinging.

"No more excuses," I said.

"Well, that's lesson one," my coach said. "Until you accept full responsibility for your results, both good and bad, you cannot make money in this business."

"OK," was all I could croak out. I felt as if I had just gone 12 rounds, and it had only been a few minutes.

In the next 12 months I sold 42 homes, doing exactly what I was told to do. I quickly moved into the top 5% of realtors. What my coach told me then and later was often hard to hear, but it made me hundreds of thousands of dollars that year. The money was more than adequate to salve my wounds.

Remember, the reason you have this person in your life is to guide and assist you in achieving your goals. Their goal should not be simply to be a cheerleader for you. Your success will be all the cheering section you will need. Yourself-worth and dignity, not to mention the money you make, will be the reward for your hard work. That does not mean that your mentor won't give you praise for things well done; however, it does mean that in your conversations with them you will find a lot more hard things to hear than easy comments to warm your heart.

If you are unwilling to listen to your mentors, do not be surprised when they have less and less time to assist you. No one wants to feel they are wasting their time on a lost cause. Don't let that cause be you.

Conversely, you may find that your mentor is unable to spend the time necessary to help you, or you may outgrow your mentor and need to look for someone who has accomplished even more. That is not a time for sadness. Rather, it's a time for joyful reflection on your accomplishments. Remember to thank those who have given of themselves to help you.

You cannot make it on your own. People will either push you up or tear you down in life, and your mentors, by their very generosity in sharing their experience, have pushed you up. You should do the same for others. No matter where you are in life you have accomplished more, lived through more, learned more than someone else. You should use those skills to mentor others. That's called "paying it forward," and there is no better way to solidify concepts in your mind than to teach them to someone else.

THOUGHTS ON MENTORS

- Everyone needs a coach or a mentor to keep them on the path.
- Just because someone claims to be an expert does not make it so.
- Look for those who have accomplished more, and develop a mentoring relationship with them as you proceed on your journey.

- Find someone willing to give you a pat on the shoulder or a kick in the pants as needed.
- Seek mentors who have accomplished what you wish to accomplish.
- Persistence pays when seeking a mentor—just short of a restraining order.
- Mentors are not your friends.
- Mentors are there to expand your mind and guide your actions.
- Realize that most of what you're going to get from a mentor is constructive criticism and guidance, not a pat on the head.
- A mentor is a sounding board, an idea generator and a problem solver—someone to help you think outside of the box in which your limited experience causes you to live.
- If you're sensitive to criticism, toughen up.
- If you're argumentative, learn a little humility and listen.
- The guidance of a mentor can shorten the path to success by decades.
- One of your goals should be to accomplish more than your mentor.
- Be grateful to those who have helped you. Speak good things into their lives.
- Teaching something is the best way to really learn it.
- Giving back is important to your success, so take the time to mentor others who haven't yet made it as far as you.

CHAPTER 13

LISTENING

So when you are listening to somebody, completely, attentively, then you are listening not only to the words, but also to the feeling of what is being conveyed, to the whole of it, not part of it.

— *Jiddu Krishnamurti*

As a type-A personality, listening has always been one of the challenging aspects of my life. Once I stopped being in a hurry to speak, my relationships improved and my success went up. Often people will continue to speak, giving you information that is useful, if you will simply give up the need to interject and instead listen. The phrase that has served me well is, "It isn't what people say, it is how they say it." For me, listening is always a work in progress.

When I was a partner in a New Horizons Computer Learning Center I had ample opportunity to hone my listening skills. Within any organization there are always interactions amongst the various departments which can lead to friction, jealousy, and in some cases, overt attempts to undermine another department. When I saw those types of interactions occurring, it was a sure sign that I had not been listening closely enough to hear what was truly being said.

One of these frictions became very obvious when one of our less discreet sales people spoke to the instructors about how much money they were making. The sales people were on 100% commission, and while several of them were making six figures, the attrition rate in the sales department was high. Spending eight hours on the phones is difficult, and you earn your money. The instructors, on the other hand, started in the 25K-30K range, with technical instructors making 50K or more.

Word of the instructors grumbling had worked its way to my office. I was contemplating what to do about it when Colleen, their supervisor, stopped by. "Tom, the instructors are complaining about how much they are paid compared to the sales people. They feel we wouldn't even have a company if they weren't in the classroom teaching."

Knowing that I would have to deal with it or have a full-scale revolt on my hands, possibly losing good instructors and certainly undermining morale, I asked her to schedule a meeting with the instructional team for the next morning. That brief delay gave me a bit of time to listen to my inner voices. My first gut reaction was to be aggressive and confrontational, but that lasted only briefly. Thinking back to the types of personalities involved in both the instructional and sales teams, I realized a softer approach was going to be necessary for the instructors.

The next morning we sat down with our 12 instructors to air out their grievances. Wanting a visual aid to assist me, I asked them to list their complaints and I would put them on the blackboard. I wanted to see if there was a common theme. The words came fast and from all participants: "more hours than the sales people," "we have more education than the sales people," "the sales people shouldn't make any more than us." For 15 minutes I filled the blackboard.

In any group there is always an opinion leader, and in this group it was Greg. "So it looks like your concerns center around the compensation package," I said, looking directly at Greg as I said it. All eyes glanced in Greg's direction to see what he would say. Greg nodded his assent.

"Well, let's explore what we can and can't do to make things better for you." At this point I was wondering what they had discussed amongst themselves, as they seemed to have a bit of an agenda. Suggestions flowed, including bonus pay, greater salaries, more time off, less classroom time, more class prep time. I filled the second blackboard. Then a comment from the room caught my attention. "Man, those sales guys got it easy."

Bingo, the gear slipped into place. "So what I hear you saying is that instructing is a tougher job then selling." Assent murmured through the room. Setting aside their suggestions for a moment, I confirmed what they were thinking one more time. "So the sales people are overpaid for what they do?" They all nodded and murmured agreement.

"I would like to make a proposal. I would like your team to come up with a couple of concrete proposals for a bonus structure for getting students to sign up for more training. You have them for six hours, you're building the rapport with them, and if you can convince them to do more training we will work out a bonus program for you." Heads nodded, and the mood lightened.

"I would like to make another proposal. I am willing to let any of you try working in sales if you think that would be a better fit for you. If you don't like it, you won't be fired; you can simply return to the instructor team. That way if you like sales and are good at it, you can make lots more money." That went over big. I wondered how many would take me up on the offer. "But," I added, "before you can switch teams you have to spend one full day on the phones, listening to a sales person make calls. Of course we will pay you for that."

Our system allowed for online monitoring and we used it for training. Now we were going to use it to show people their options. The meeting ended with several instructors asking to listen in on the phones.

What the instructors were saying was not that they were really mad that the successful sales people were making great money. They felt the work was not worth the pay. By carefully listening to their concerns we were able to actually develop a bonus program that allowed the instructors to make up to 20% more if a certain number of their students took additional training. Moreover, several instructors spent their day on the phone—and were appalled at how they were treated. Phone sales is a challenging business, and after listening to the rejection and the work necessary to bring in a client, none of the instructors changed teams. None left the store over the pay, either, and the respect and camaraderie amongst the teams was greatly improved.

As you recover from your current situation you are going to need to do so through your relationships with other people. Mary Morrisey, a spiritual and dream coach, says that listening is the highest form of love. You should seek to learn about others and build a relationship with them through really listening to them, putting the focus of your attention completely on them. Studies have shown that when someone is asked to repeat what a person has just said to them moments before, most can only list a fraction of what was said. That's because they weren't really listening; they were just waiting to talk.

There is a huge difference between listening and waiting to talk. When you are truly listening you are living in the moment; you are focused not only on what the other person is saying, but also on their demeanor and body language, which are important cues to the full meaning of their words. When you truly listen to another without trying to formulate a response in your mind at the same time, it sends a signal to that person that you believe they are important, and that what they are saying is valuable to you. This simple step will start to change the relationships in your life.

When you fail to listen with attention, your demeanor changes. You stand differently; you look at the person with whom you're speaking differently; you move your head differently. All these cues are picked up by the person with whom you are speaking. They may not even realize it consciously, but unconsciously they know you are not listening to them. Studies have shown that the vast majority of communication is nonverbal, so what message are you sending?

You will find this one thing will vastly improve your business and personal life. There are many old sayings surrounding listening, but I think two bear repeating. The first saying is, "People don't care what you say until they know that you care." How can you demonstrate that you care about the other person? I believe that the number one way is by listening. People are yearning to be heard, to be understood, to be recognized as important. When you listen carefully to what people are saying you will be amazed at what you hear. Watch the body language, listen to the tone of voice, note how they move their hands and body. What are they really saying? The words will convey a meaning, but what else is their body telling you? When you learn not only to listen with your ears but also to read the other person's mannerisms, you will have learned to truly listen. You will be far more in tune with what is really being said.

The second saying is, "You have two ears and one mouth, and you should use them in that proportion." When you listen more than speak, you are often thought wise and reflective. When you listen to what the other person is saying completely and without interruption, only then taking the time to formulate a response, others will elevate your stature in their own mind.

As you work to rebuild your business and your life, this one simple thing will change relationships, heal old wounds, and propel you forward. If you're the one who usually does all the talking others will take notice. As I spoke less and listened more I was often asked if I was OK. I would respond that yes, I was fine; I was simply listening to what they had to say. There would often be an incredulous look as if I had told them something truly profound. I could feel the energy of our interaction changing immediately. The people to whom you are speaking will consider you not only wise and reflective but worthy of their time, willing to learn, willing to consider the advice and thoughts of others.

Even if you do not follow their advice, or respond in the manner which they had hoped, their reaction will be much more positive. We have all had the experience of saying something to someone where we get the feeling they are just waiting for us to finish so they can speak. You feel as if they are telling you "My time is more valuable than yours, so could you please finish so I can speak or get out of this conversation?" Even if you get the response you wanted from that person, how do you feel about the interaction? Are you positive, enthusiastic, and happy, or are do you feel disrespected, unimportant, and distrustful?

Think back to how you listen. What message are you sending out to those around you? Perhaps, like me, you have been the boss. You simply expect people to do as you say without question. Ask yourself:

how are your relationships? Maybe you listen in one part of your life and fail to listen in others. How might your business and personal relationships change for the better if you took the time to listen?

Your message will change from one of disdain for the other person to one of inclusiveness, warmth, understanding, and consideration of the other person's point of view. Instead of people speaking badly about you behind your back you will find champions in your corner. Those with whom you interact will speak good things about you, and good things will happen in your life. Over time, your advice and council will be sought out and valued, you will be looked to as a leader, a mentor, and as a person worthy of respect and trust.

This has been an area in which I have personally struggled. I often wish people would pick up the pace as there is so much to be done. I have been accused of being nice to people but aloof, of being lost in my own world, oblivious to those around me. The fact of the matter is, the people who made those accusations were right. Perhaps you can relate when I say that sometimes I begin to believe in my own importance a little too much and ignore what others are saying. Now, you are almost certainly not going to say that to someone with whom you have a personal or business relationship, are you? But you don't need to tell them; it comes through in the way you listen. As I have worked to improve my listening skills my own relationships have improved, and so will yours.

The essence of leadership is persuading people to follow you willingly. Many entrepreneurs hold their teams together with the force of their personalities. However, if it is the force of your personality or the paycheck you provide, your growth is going to be limited. Listening will set you up as the leader for whom others work willingly to accomplish your vision. These people will grow your business, watch your back, and when setbacks happen they will help you come back stronger and better than you have ever been. Truly listening is such a simple thing, but it has the potential by itself to create better relationships, financial riches, and internal joy and contentment.

THOUGHTS ON LISTENING

- People sense when you are not listening.
- Listening is focused attention on the person speaking.
- People love and respect those who can listen attentively.
- Do not think about your response while listening or you will miss what is truly being said.
- Real listening pays attention not only to the words spoken but rather in the way they are said.
- Your stature and perceived intelligence will grow based on your ability to listen.
- Your mentors and coaches are people you respect—listen carefully to what they say.
- Listen with your eyes as well as your ears. What is the body language telling you?
- You have two ears and one mouth and they should be used in that proportion.
- One who listens to others is seldom thought a fool.
- When you listen, people learn to trust and respect you.
- With trust and respect your business will grow.
- When you listen, your personal relationships will blossom.
- Listening makes the other person feel important.
- Those who feel you truly listen to them will be your champions and will speak good about you and into your life.

- Since everything you want will come from your relationships to others, simply listening has the potential to create massive success in your life.
- People have a need to be heard; when you provide that need your opportunities will multiply.

CHAPTER 14

WHERE DO I GO FROM HERE?

One Machine can do the work of fifty ordinary men. No machine can do the work of one extraordinary man.
— *Elbert Hubbard*

When I and my friend Roger were 12 years old, I started working on his family farm after school and during the summers. We've been close ever since. Roger and his wife Sherri, whom he met when he was 16, eventually owned one of the largest farming operations in the Midwest. With no formal schooling beyond high school, Roger has more brains and better judgment than most college graduates. He is the poster boy for what hard work, good sense and a great wife can do for you.

After many years of farming, though, Roger and Sherri had enough. As he put it, "You put two million in the ground and if things go well you make a six figure income. If things go badly you go broke." So Roger and Sherri sold their farm, relocated to Texas and bought a semi rig. Now Roger drives his truck with little stress, a great income, and money in the bank. He is one relaxed individual. He had been inviting me for years to ride along with him, and since I had a lot more time than money, that is exactly what I did: spend some quality time with my oldest friend.

"Rog, thanks for letting me ride along on this run." I was looking forward to getting some time to talk. Even though we remained close, living 1,500 miles apart doesn't make for regular contact.

"No problem. Hope you know what you're in for. We're heading up to Oklahoma, then across to Illinois, up into Wisconsin, and then back to Texas." Jeez, and he does this every week. People say I am crazy but he just has this silly grin on his face. He loves it—he's his own boss with low stress and a great payday.

"How do you sit in this truck and do the same route every week?" I was sure my butt would give out long before my attitude.

"I find it relaxing. I know where I'm going; I just take my time, and the money is good." Well, he did spend a fortune on that great seat. I was envious. Having seen him work hard under enormous stress, I was glad to see he was happy.

"Good for you, glad things have worked out so nicely for you and Sherri. You guys work your ass off and deserve it." Had he kept farming he would have probably joined his dad in a very early grave. I was thrilled to see how happy he seemed to be.

"So, what are your plans?"

We had about 3,000 miles to talk about this. He would probably want to jump out of the truck before the trip was over, with me yammering non-stop the whole way.

"I don't know. I guess since I'm starting over I have options. One of my friends offered me a great job, making nice money, but I just can't see myself in car sales or as a manager again. One of the advantages of starting over is I know where I went wrong the first time and I won't be that stupid again." My perspective had been changing. Going broke had been unpleasant, but it wasn't as bad as I thought it would be. I had worked myself into a corner and there was no way out. I was going to be stuck right where I was for 10 years or more. Then I went broke, and suddenly I was free again.

Free to rebuild with the knowledge I had gained. Free to do whatever I wanted and with the foresight to avoid the pitfalls which caused me to stumble last time. As time passed I felt more and more fortunate.

"Hey, lots of guys went bust. Of course, you did it with style and in a big way." Roger smiled. He was yanking my chain, but with more than a little truth.

"Thanks for the vote of confidence." I said with a hint of sarcasm. After all, that scar tissue could still hurt a tiny bit when poked.

"Hey, we almost went under ourselves." Farming is tough business. When it is good it is good, when it is bad, it is horrible.

"Well if you're going to go down it doesn't pay to do it half way now does it? Go big or go home."

"There's the spirit!" He really shouldn't be egging me on. He knew I'd just keep going.

"Well I know what I don't want, so now I just have to decide what it is I do want. I definitely want a check coming in every month whether I show up or not. Guess that means I am working for myself, but I want to build something that is actually a business instead of a job. I thought

I had a business but if I didn't show up and put sales on the board nothing happened. Way too much grief. And I am really not very interested in employees." Roger always thought I was one sandwich short of a picnic. He and Sherri would laugh about my adventures and business ventures. But I think they enjoyed seeing what I was up to.

"Don't want much, do you?" Always the master of the understatement, that Roger.

"If I'm going to rebuild something I am going to do it right this time. The heck with convention; I'm not going to follow the rest of the lemmings off the cliff. When I see where the rest of the sheep are going, I just figure the opposite way is better."

I could feel my stress dropping with every mile that passed. And as we talked the hours away, I began to see where I was going next.

When someone asks you what you want out of life, do you know? Have you ever even admitted it to yourself? Well, it's time to get honest with yourself and figure it out. There are entire books written on determining what it is you want out of life, and if you need the help, then by all means buy one of those books or CD courses.

After my bankruptcy I spent time in reflection out on my own, either hiking, or sometimes just sitting and contemplating what it is important to me in life. One of the techniques I used was to ask myself how I wanted to be remembered when I am gone. What do you want people to say about you? Great friend and father or mother—wonderful wife or husband—incredible business person—loved by the community—made a difference in world—donated large sums to worthwhile causes—traveled the world—did it their way—people looked up to them. What would you like your legacy to be?

You need to ask yourself if you want to rebuild in the same line of business that you had previously. If you're going to make a change, now is the time. Since you have probably experienced tremendous setbacks if you're reading this now, I urge you to take some time to honestly decide if what you did in the past is what you want to do in the future.

Why is it you have been doing what you have been doing? My parents did it, so I do it—it's what I went to school for—it's all I know how to do—I would have to move to find work—my family expects it of me—I have bills to pay—I need the security of a paycheck—I need benefits for myself or my family—I've tried and failed before. I've probably heard hundreds of excuses in my day and I have used most of them at one point or another, but those excuses do not serve you, they hinder you.

Does what you do give you satisfaction and a sense of purpose, or are you stuck in cubicle hell, pushing paper and just waiting for the clock to hit quitting time? Will what you are doing now, or what you were previously doing, give you the lifestyle you desire? Will it allow you to spend time with your family or travel, if that is your goal? Will you make the kind of income you deserve? Can your position or business provide a lifestyle for those you love and care for?

I say this with love, having been in your shoes myself, but it is time to give yourself a not so gentle kick in the butt as a wake-up call. You know you were born for something better than this, and so do I. God, the universe or whatever higher power you believe in wants you to be happy. Forget all this hogwash about suffering on earth for your reward in heaven. You have an obligation to yourself, your family, and frankly to society, to succeed. The best thing you can do for your family is to provide well for them, and the best thing you can do for society is to not be a burden on it.

Life will give you what you demand of it. Demand plenty. If you believe you are too old, too stupid, too poor, or have failed too many times to be able to get out of your rut, then you're right. The first place you are going to have to work is in your head. As long as the six inches of real estate between your ears is negative on you, life will be negative for you. But as long as you're pushing air in and out of your lungs you can learn, change, adapt, and succeed.

THOUGHTS ON WHERE TO GO FROM HERE

- Is where you are where you want to rebuild?
- Is where you are today going to provide the type of income you deserve?
- If your current position doesn't meet your financial goals, can it be adapted to do so?
- If your current position doesn't meet your lifestyle goals, can it be modified without making major changes to better serve your life?
- It is often better to start in the business you know and make it serve you, branching out from there as you develop cash flow.
- If you are set on making a move now the time is now, you're starting over anyway.
- Be successful. You deserve it, your family deserves it, and your society needs it!
- Life will give you what you demand of it and work for.
- How do you want to be remembered?

- It's time to take yourself to the woodshed for a kick in the pants to get you moving again on a better course toward your better life.

CHAPTER 15

THE PERFECTION TRAP

People throw away what they could have by insisting on perfection, which they cannot have, and looking for it where they will never find it.

— Edith Schaeffer

As the owner of a technology-based company, I had more than my fair share of perfectionists working for me. The personality required to sit and write computer code day after day lends itself to perfectionism. But if you want to accomplish something great you need to learn when good enough is good enough.

"Tom, it's not perfect. I can make it better." Mike, our technical guru, was adamant that the program he had written to manage our training center needed more work.

"I understand that, Mike." *We had this same conversation last week*, I thought to myself.

"Another couple of weeks and we should be ready to test it." Mike was almost pleading.

"How about this?" I said. "We go live tomorrow and work out the bugs from there." I thought Mike was going to throw up on my desk. He had gone completely ashen.

"That's impossible," he sputtered in dismay.

"Nothing is impossible," I countered. "We will never know where the problems are until we start using it. Once we are using it you will know what to tweak and what to leave alone." I was wishing I had a Valium in my desk for the poor guy. He looked like he had lost his last friend.

"Mike," I went on to explain, "You have done a great job. It will never be perfect and it's a waste of time and money to try to make it perfect. At some point you've done all you can. Now it's time to kick your baby out of the crib and make it walk." Mike's head hung low; I knew that he truly believed he could make it better. He was probably right. But I also knew that if I let him, he would spend months if not years trying to make it perfect, and by the time it met his standard of perfection it would already be obsolete.

"What if it doesn't work right?" Mike said with fear in his voice.

"Then you will fix it—right?" Mike nodded in the affirmative. "Relax Mike! We just need something that works for now, and I know if there are any issues you can take care of them. I have complete faith in you." That brought a little smile.

"Thanks," Mike said. "I guess I had better get to work. It's going to be a long couple of days."

The next day we launched. As expected, there were quite a few bugs, but Mike quickly tracked them down and fixed the problems. He was as happy as could be, jumping from problem to problem, fixing this, fixing that. Within a week we were humming, everything working like a charm.

Mike stopped by my office the next week. "Tom, I thought you were nuts. I didn't think it would ever work."

"Well," I responded, "the technology is changing so fast that it doesn't need to be perfect. Heck, Microsoft has made an industry out of putting out technology with bugs that need to be fixed."

Mike laughed. "I have a couple ideas for improvements." He outlined some creative updates to improve processing.

"Sounds great," I said. "How long for the first update?"

"I should be able to crank it out in a month."

"We launch in two weeks," I told him.

Mike made a fuss but left the office with a smile on his face. I thought to myself, *he must have doubled the time he thought it would take. I hate it when I am predictable. Well, if that was the case Mike played his hand well. Have to give him credit, and the time I promised. Next time—one week*

You will often hear people speak of perfection. Perfection is the enemy of success and achievement.

Since you have probably failed at something, it's only natural to try to make things perfect the next time around. I have also learned that good enough is good enough. The key is to get started, whether or not everything is perfect in your business, your attitude, or your life. A plan is important, but a perfect plan that you never put into action will take you nowhere. It won't put a dollar in the bank, food on the table, or generate the lifestyle you desire. You will never have perfect knowledge, so a perfect plan is not even a real possibility. A mediocre plan implemented with energy and belief will get you into motion, and even if you turn out to be on the wrong path, it's easier to change direction than it is to start from a dead stop. Go as far as you can see. When you get there, you will be able to see farther and adjust course as necessary.

Perfection is a cocoon in which unsuccessful people wrap themselves. When you have to have perfect bookkeeping, a perfectly organized office, a perfect business plan or a perfect anything you never have to face getting started. You can continually postpone your start date until things are perfect so you never have to face the reality that success is often messy, and filled with uncertainty and even failure.

The idea that you have to be perfect is comfortable, because you never have to truly start anything, much less finish. If you don't start you don't have to face the fact that things may not go perfectly. When you look deep inside yourself, you'll find that perfection is a protection mechanism for your ego and your self-image. If you never start, it is always possible to fool yourself by saying, "I could have done that if I had wanted to," or perhaps, "The timing just wasn't right," or "That would never work in my area." These thoughts are self-sabotaging.

As Loral Langemeier says in her book *Yes Energy,* it's not about perfection, it's about commitment. The results you want in your life need to be the driving force of your action. When you obsess on perfection, obstacles are avoided or denied, rather than faced. "Good enough" creates action that can be improved. Playing small serves no one and it is selfish not to share your gifts with the world. Find successful people and model them. You'll quickly discover that they aren't perfect.

I understand the desire to have things perfect, especially when things have blown up in your face in the past. It's easy to plan to plan, to generate reams of paper, tons of charts, and dream of what someday may be. I also realize that you will not get back on your feet, or realize any important goals, if you need things to be perfect. All successful people accept that there is going to be a certain level of ambiguity in their personal and work lives, and you need to accept that truth, too.

I truly believe that the drive to perfection is largely based on your personality type. Generally the more introspective, the more analytical you are, the more concerned you are about getting things perfect. If you are an outgoing, type A personality, your problem isn't perfection, it's more likely failing to look at all before you leap. Either one can cause problems, but action tends to overcome problems while perfectionism creates an environment where the problems never surface because nothing is ever done.

If you are highly analytical, with a driving need to perfection, it is time to start setting some deadlines. Set a period for planning, gather as much information as you can in the time allotted, and move forward. If you fail to do this you will continue to generate reams of data, all of which is going to be obsolete by the time you reach your level of comfort. By then something else will happen to make you uncomfortable, generating further delays. Eventually either you lose interest or someone beats you to your goal and you lose the prize—again.

Set time lines and stick to them. Making planning a part of your daily activity once you begin your project or business, not an endless activity done in lieu of ever starting. You can make things better, but until you actually begin something—start selling a product, speaking to customers, or doing something to put money in the bank—you will not find the weaknesses in your plan.

In any endeavor you are aiming for a moving target. You need to develop a belief in yourself and in your ability to adapt. I believe the drive to perfection shows a lack of confidence in your own ability and it is manifested in the need for more information and more planning, one feeding off the other in a never-ending circle that ends only in disappointment.

You can use your perfectionist impulses to make changes to your venture as it begins to bring in cash. Your goal of perfection is helpful here, as you work for the incremental improvements which to put even more money on the bottom line. Just be sure to focus on the money-making activities. Perfectionists like to spend time on non-profit-making activities. Drive it home into your brain: no profit, no business; no business, and you might as well go golfing.

When you direct a perfectionist mentality into the profit-making activities of a business, you can drive some serious growth into that business. I have two suggestions here. First, if you are a perfectionist you should focus on being a sales and marketing perfectionist. Those are the activities that bring cash in the door. The perfectionists among you will probably go into shock at the abomination of my second suggestion. Contract out almost everything.

I can hear the screams of agony across the country. "But I can do it myself," you're saying. Perhaps; and perhaps you can do it better than anyone else. Nonetheless, unless you want to work 24 hours a day, with no freedom, a business that won't grow, and a family that doesn't recognize you, dump the stuff you are not flat-out incredible at doing. Use Virtual Assistants or hire someone to do everything (and I do mean everything!) else. Your perfectionist traits, when properly focused on the things that make you money, can leapfrog you into success. But ONLY when you focus narrowly on what's most important for your business and learn to let good enough be good enough for everything else.

Realize that if you stumble you can get back on course. There are many paths to success, and one of the paths often taken is the path of failure. While you may know someone who has hit it big the first time, that's not generally how success happens. Overnight success isn't necessarily a blessing, either. It can raise resentment or jealousy, and further embed the need for perfection in your mind. If you are like most successful people you have failed often enough, fallen down and gotten back up enough times to learn what you need to know to be successful. Stop being ashamed or embarrassed that you're not perfect, and get into action.

THOUGHTS ON THE PERFECTION TRAP

- You're not perfect—accept it.
- Pursuit of perfection will guarantee your perfect failure.
- Pursuit of perfection allows you to hide from reality.
- Be honest with yourself, even if with no one else; face your fears.
- Success isn't based on being perfect; it is based on being imperfect and adjusting course as you go.
- Your personality type can make it easier or harder for you to start moving.
- Set deadlines for actually moving forward and limit planning.
- Over planning is worse than no planning.
- Long-term planning generates very little additional data that is of use.

- The world is changing fast, so slow plans are obsolete before they are complete.
- Have or develop confidence in yourself by taking action.
- Perfectionists can make incredible gains if they keep the end in mind and move forward.
- Perfection, narrowly focused, can drive incremental gains.
- If you must focus on perfection, focus on those things that put money in the bank; hire the rest out and get started.

CHAPTER 16

TIME TO BEGIN ANEW

Twenty years from now you will more disappointed by the things you didn't do than by the ones you did do. So throw off the bowlines, sail away from the safe harbor. Catch the trade winds in your sails. Explore. Dream, Discover.

— *Mark Twain*

Pain of discipline is temporary; the pain of compromise is permanent.

- *Joel Osteen*

Read these quotes again and contemplate the meaning. Let the words sink deep into your mind. Life is not a dress rehearsal for something else; it is your one and only chance to live the life you dream of living. Be unafraid to truly consider what it is you really want.

Planning is important, but the best plan in the world is worth nothing as long as it sits on paper or in your head. Plans only have value when they are executed. I have friends and business acquaintances who have been planning a business for a decade or more. They can visualize it in their mind, but they have never been able to move ahead. You must set a time limit on your planning, and then move into the execution phase. If you refuse to do this you may as well save your time, since what you're really doing is an exercise in dreaming.

My problem is the opposite. I am quick to jump into new ventures, often without taking the time to plan. Over time I have learned difficult lessons when my failure to plan led me down the wrong path. Planning is a vital tool for success. Just don't get stuck at the drawing board.

The first priority in planning is to picture the outcome. What do you want to accomplish? How will it look when you're done? What role do you want to play in the business? Once you know how it will look in the end you should determine where you are now. Then it's simply a matter of mapping out the steps between your present position and your destination. Always keeping the end in mind will guide you in your daily, monthly, and yearly activities as you advance step by step toward your goal.

How do you eat an elephant? One bite at a time. Your goals should be broken down into weekly or even daily steps. This allows you to accomplish something each day or week, even if it is a small thing. Human nature causes us to lose interest and motivation as we stretch out the timeline for completion of a project. The universe loves action. Your idea wasn't just given to you alone; it was given to others who may act more quickly than you if you don't jump on it. All of us have had the experience of seeing a product or service and saying to ourselves, "I thought of that years ago," yet we failed to act and someone else did. Isn't it time you acted on your inspirations?

"I want a business that I can run from anywhere, so it has to be able to be run over the internet." My coach Will was listening.

"Well, do you have a niche in which you want to work?" Will asked.

I replied, "I do. I want to start coaching new investors so they don't make any expensive mistakes on their first deals."

"That sounds like a good niche," Will responded. "I coach others who work in real estate but no one is focusing on the beginning investor."

I proceeded to speak for several minutes about my plans, all the items I needed to have in place before I started. I elaborated on the website, marketing, target market; on and on. Will listened patiently till I paused for breath.

"And how much will you be making from your business during all this?" he asked.

"Ummm, nothing I guess."

"But you will be spending large sums to get up and running, am I right?" I hate it when someone points out the flaws in my plan, but I had to admit he was right.

"Yeah, I guess so," I said slowly, a bit dejected.

Will heard it in my voice. "I am not saying you shouldn't do it. I think you should do all of it, but it could take months, maybe a year to get everything perfected, and in that time you will be bleeding cash every day. You will never get to the point of launching your business, because you will already be broke or so discouraged that you quit." I responded with a grunt. Will continued, "Why don't we launch within 30 days and start earning some cash now? It doesn't need to be perfect; it just needs to be making you money. You can use the money to improve things as you go. You'll be making a living at the same time you're able to use your cash flow to keep making incremental improvements."

"You know, that does make sense." I was wondering how I was going to pay for everything when I was putting the plan together.

"It will pay for itself if you do it right. Planning is no substitute for action." Wow, first coaching session with this guy and he already has me focusing on the cash. Start with a basic plan and then make improvements—what a concept! Wish I had thought of that.

"Here's what we are going to do. . ." and I was off and running.

It's time to get down to some more direct action steps. Let's ask a few questions to see where you are and where you want to go. I am going to suggest you pull out a pad of paper and write down some thoughts as you go. Don't judge the thoughts, just put down what comes to your mind. And as always, the most important thing is to be honest with yourself.

What is it that is important to you in your life?

The most critical question you need to answer is: what do you value? Not what society values, what your friends value or even what your family values. What do you value? What do you care about more than anything? Family, Great Achievement, Public Service, Travel, Lifestyle—you need to choose, and you can choose more than one. You simply need to prioritize them in order of importance.

Most people have never done this simple step, often because they are afraid to admit, even to themselves, what they really want. They have been conditioned by society to believe they need to answer this question in a way that will satisfy others' expectations. The only thing you need to decide, and answer, is what do *you* want? Set down the baggage of your past life, the baggage thrust upon you by society and your family and just be you.

The most loving thing you can do for yourself is to stop lying to yourself. Face the truth of what it is that is important to you, and set yourself free to reach for it.

Do you want to remake your life into what you had before, or something different?

If you have honestly answered question one, question two should almost answer itself. Knowing what's important in your life will guide your actions as you begin this new journey.

As you get older your priorities change. Twenty years from now what you considered important may be meaningless to you. Time changes things, and it changes you, it's part of growth. At a certain age, when there is less time ahead of you than behind, your perspective changes. You tend to care less about what others think you should do. Maturity provides the experience to help you determine your future path at this fork in your life's journey.

You do not need to be older to have this lack of concern for society's conventions, or the opinions of you family and friends. It can be developed at any age when you begin to believe in yourself. Allow no one to steer you in your decision. If your desires lean toward regaining what you previously had, let no one tell you differently. If, on the other hand, you wish to wind up at a different destination, then chart your course for your new promised land. Listen to your heart and let your head find a way.

This was one of the areas in which I personally struggled. If you have talent and abilities the world of possibilities is wide open to you. With the virtually unlimited number of options available, yet with limited life, what do you truly want to devote your energies, your talents, and the years of your life to accomplishing? You can rebuild in the same business or job, or you can change. You can stay in the same community or move. You can live in the same country or expand your horizons. What excites you? What possibilities motivate you? What thoughts thrill you? Are you confident or fearful? You must let the past go, regain your confidence, and accept what comes as a normal part of life.

Have you defined how you want your life to look when you have accomplished your goals?

Imagine yourself with your goals fulfilled. How does it feel? What does your life look like? Who are the people in your life? Where are you living and how are you making your living? What emotions go through your body when you imagine living in your wishes-fulfilled universe? Contentment, confidence, joy, peace, satisfaction, self-worth? Write down what it feels like to be there.

Interestingly, most people will never commit their goals to paper. Yet this small step is critical in your the development of your future. Why? Because it begins to tell your subconscious mind that you are serious about success. When you tell yourself you wish to change yet you take no positive steps to make it happen your subconscious mind does not trust you and therefore does nothing to help, or even sabotages your efforts.

You have to trust yourself. You have to say what it is you want and begin to take steps toward the realization of that life. Any step, even a small step done on a consistent basis, will help bring good things into your life. Until you are ready to be faithful in the small things you need to do to recover and prosper you will not see the great things in your future.

Are you willing to set down the baggage of the past, forgiving yourself and others for mistakes and hurts so that you can move ahead into this new life you desire?

Who are you hurting by holding onto the past? You're hurting yourself and those around you who deserve better from you. You cannot change the past. You can only use it as a guide to keep you out of trouble in the future. You cannot hold two opposite feelings in your mind simultaneously and achieve success. You cannot be confident yet fearful, happy but sad, jealous but content, forgiven yet unforgiving. Love yourself with all your faults. Forgive others for their faults. Set down the burdens you have been carrying; it's OK. The world forgives and the world forgets.

How can you monetize your goals? What can you do to create the lifestyle you say you desire?

Money buys peace of mind. It may not buy happiness, but the lack of money probably creates more stress in your life than anything else. When you have money in the bank, when you're not concerned about how the bills will be paid or how you're going to survive till your next paycheck, life takes on a whole new glow.

Speaking from experience from both sides of the wealth coin, if you have never had the peace of mind in your life that money provides, you owe it to yourself to experience it. If you have had money in your life you know the peace of mind it provides. When you wake up each morning, your problems seem smaller and your life seems filled with more options.

If you know what is important, and you know what you want for your life, how can you make it put money in the bank? Brainstorm ideas that will allow you to achieve the lifestyle you want. Read books or go online to explore your options (I have provided a number of book resources in the back of this book which may assist you. You can also visit the resource page my website www.YouAreTough.com for more ideas.). Focus on generating revenue, not on busy work which brings in no money. The busy work is unnecessary until you actually have money to worry about.

If you have no cash you need to focus on immediate cash flow. Get Loral Langemeier's book *Put More Cash In Your Pocket* for some quick cash flow ideas. You need to combine immediate practicality with a look to the future. You won't be able to focus on your dreams if you're worried about eating tomorrow. You don't need to love what it is you do short term for cash; you simply need to bring in the money. Once you have cash flow begin immediately to implement your future plan.

If you want things in your life to change, you have to change the things in your life. So simple. So hard. Are you ready to do the hard work, to try again, to rekindle the spirit that lies within you?

I wish I could say it would be easy, that success is guaranteed this time, but that would not be reality. Reality is, for you to have what you say you desire in your life, you have to change. The battle back to success and happiness is waged almost entirely in your mind. Henry Ford said it well: "If you think you can, or you think you can't, you're right." Where did you make mistakes before? Use those as signposts to stay off that road and try to avoid the same mistakes again. Do not let your concerns about mistakes paralyze you into inactivity. You will make new mistakes. Let them be the gentle tap on the arm to help you adjust course.

Are you motivated by love or hate?

Love is positive energy; hate is negative energy. If you give it free reign, hate will consume you and affect those who are foolish enough to be anywhere near you. When you are around people who are constantly negative you can actually feel the anger radiating from their body. It doesn't matter if the hate is directed inward or outward; the effect is the same.

It is easier to be negative than it is to be positive. Have you ever heard or read a book on how to be negative? But even though hate is easier, it less powerful than love. You must rise above any hate, both for yourself and others, to find contentment.

You must love yourself in order to give love to others. Love will carry you further. It will magnify your successes and minimize your failures. Love will provide comfort in the bad times and multiply your joy in the good times.

You cannot give away what you do not have. If you don't love and respect yourself how can you give love and respect to others? You must develop a deep-seated love of yourself so that you may give it away to others. When you love yourself, your energy changes. You exude confidence, joy, contentment; very attractive features which will draw people and circumstances into your life that will help you back on the road to your success.

Your future is found in your own mind. What you have or don't have is a function of what you think about day in and day out. The actions you take, day in and day out. What you believe about yourself and others, day in and day out.

You can build a castle or live in a cave depending on the six inches between your ears. What holds good people back is nothing more than an illusion, a collection of thoughts which have forced them into their present circumstances. Only you can change your thoughts and thus your future. No one can get in your mind with a pick ax and shovel and dig out those thoughts which are undermining your success. Only you can do that. Begin today to let go of the past and move into the future. The universe wants you to be happy. God wants you to be happy. Do you want to be happy and content? Do the work necessary and good things will begin to happen in your life.

By this point it is my hope and prayer that you have started to put your life, and even your failures, into perspective. I have found that every time I read a book I pick up new things, new perspectives that I missed the first time. Perhaps unlocking the vault to your mind takes time. When you read something once the vault opens slightly. With each successive re-reading new treasures are found. Put this book aside, but only for a time. Revisit it in the near future. The universe has great expectations of you, and great things in store for you. It does require you to ask for what you want, focus on what you want, and work toward what you want, but it will deliver far more quickly when you follow the steps in this book.

I have provided some additional resources, which I have personally used to help myself, and which may help you, in an appendix to this book. Take the time to look through this list and select the resources which may be most helpful to you.

Look ahead with optimism and expectation. Look back with peace and acceptance. Believe once again in yourself. Be happy, be successful, be fulfilled. Know that the universe and my little corner of it are sending good karma your way on your new journey to your wishes-fulfilled life.

FINAL THOUGHTS

- Poor people give up easily and quickly saying something didn't work out. Rich people dig in and get tough. They work harder and understand everyone has setbacks and you have to power through the tough times.

- Poor people make excuses. Rich people accept responsibility for what has gone right, as well as wrong.

- Poor people accept not having their desires. Rich people won't tolerate not fulfilling their dreams.

- Poor people have poor friends who give them poor advice. They are concerned what their poor friends will say. Rich people don't care what others think, especially their poor friends, and make their own decisions.

- Poor people constantly complain. Rich people are grateful for what they do have and the opportunity to do better.

- Poor people are excited to have a job. Rich people hire them.

- Poor people drag out of bed depressed about their existence. Rich people are excited to see what the new day brings.

- Poor people think they are unlucky and the rich are lucky. The rich work hard to make themselves lucky and take advantage of the opportunities when they appear.

- Poor people always assume someone is out to take advantage of them. The rich understand that everything you want in life you have to get through your relationships with others.

- Poor people listen to the opinions of others and allow them to crush their dreams. The rich value their own opinions and dreams.

- Poor people procrastinate. Rich people take action.

- Poor people work for other people, are paid by the hour, and are concerned about security. Rich people work for themselves, are paid on their efforts, and understand the only security is what is in your mind.

- Poor people have settled for what life has handed them. Rich people grab life by the throat and shake it till it gives up what is in the heart and dreams of the rich person.

- Poor people are not teachable and if they were to make money they would quickly lose it. Rich people are always learning, always improving and are able to keep and manage what they have.

CHAPTER 17

MENTAL AMMUNITION FOR THE TOUGH DAYS

Let's face it: not every day on the road to success is sunshine and flowers. There will be more than a few days when you find your will to succeed challenged and your spirit at a low ebb. When I have those days, I find it helpful to remember that every winner faced hurdles similar to mine, and overcame them. Their lives are proof by example that success is a choice—a choice that I can make, too. Keeping their words of encouragement in my ears every day makes me feel less alone on the journey. Here are some quotes that have helped revive my spirit when it needed a boost; I hope they will do the same for you.

Only through focus can you do world class things, no matter how capable you are.

– Bill Gates

I've missed more than 9000 shots in my career. I've lost almost 300 games. Twenty-six times I've been trusted to take the game winning shot and missed. I've failed over and over again in my life. And that is why I succeed.

– Michael Jordan

The only difference between a rich person and poor person is how they use their time. The poor, the unsuccessful, the unhappy, the unhealthy are the ones who use the word tomorrow the most.

– Robert Kiyosaki

Ability is what you're capable of doing. Motivation determines what you do. Attitude determines how well you do it.

– Lou Holtz

If you can imagine it, you can achieve it; if you can dream it, you can become it.

– William Arthur Ward

Live as if you were going to die tomorrow. Learn as if you were to live forever.

– Mohandas Gandhi

A man of character finds a special attractiveness in difficulty, since it is only by coming to grips with difficulty that he can realize his potentialities.

– Charles de Gaulle

The secret of success is to do the common things uncommonly well.

– John D. Rockefeller Jr.

If you wish success in life, make perseverance your bosom friend, experience your wise counselor, caution your elder brother, and hope your guardian genius.

– Joseph Addison

Do not wait; the time will never be just right.

– Napoleon Hill

Not everything that is faced can be changed. But nothing can be changed until it is faced

– James Arthur Baldwin

Fire above the mark you intend to hit. Energy, invincible determination, with the right motive, are the levers that move the world.

– Noah Porter

Avoid having your ego so close to your position that, when your position fails, your ego goes with it.

– Colin Powell

In the arena of human life, the honors and rewards fall to those who show their good qualities in action

– Aristotle

Difficulties are meant to rouse, not discourage. The human spirit is to grow strong by conflict.

– William Ellery Channing

Nobody made a greater mistake than he who did nothing because he could do only a little.

– Edmund Burke

Remember, a person who wins success may have been counted out many times before. He wins because he refused to give up.

– Kemmons Wilson

What we need is optimism, humanism, enthusiasm, intuition, curiosity, love, humor, magic, fun, and the secret ingredient – euphoria.

– Anital Roddick

Knowing others is intelligence; knowing yourself is true wisdom. Mastering others is strength; mastering yourself is true power.

– Lao Tzu

Have confidence that if you have done a little thing well, you can do a bigger thing well, too.

– David Storey

If your actions inspire others to dream more, learn more, do more and become more, you are a leader.

– John Quincy Adams

Our lives improve only when we take chances—and the first and most difficult risk we can take is to be honest with ourselves.

- Walter Anderson

One's philosophy is not best expressed in words; it is expressed in the choices one makes....In the long run, we shape our lives and we shape ourselves. The process never ends until we die. And, the choices we make are ultimately our own responsibility.

- Eleanor Roosevelt

Obstacles are those frightful things you see when you take your eyes off the goal.

– Henry Ford

Hope begins in the dark; the stubborn hope that if you just show up and try to do the right thing, the dawn will come. You wait and watch and work; you don't give up.

- Anne Lamott

I cannot give you the formula for success, but I can give you the formula for failure—which is: Try to please everybody.

– Herbert Bayard Swope

Expect to have hope rekindled. Expect your prayers to be answered in wondrous ways. The dry seasons in life do not last. The spring rains will come again.

– Sarah Ban Breathnach

It is not because things are difficult that we do not dare, it is because we do not dare that they are difficult.

– Seneca

I never thought of losing, but now that it's happened, the only thing is to do it right. That's my obligation to all the people who believe in me. We all have to take the defeats in life.

— Muhammad Ali

People do not decide to become extraordinary. They decide to accomplish extraordinary things.

— Edmund Hillary

In adversity, remember to keep an even mind.

— Horace

Pay no attention to what the critics say; no statue has ever been erected to a critic.

— Jean Sibelius

The secret of getting things done is to act.

— Dante Alighieri

The only limit of our realization of tomorrow will be our doubts of today. Let us move forward with strong and active faith.

— Franklin D. Roosevelt

Great spirits have always encountered violent opposition from mediocre minds.

— Albert Einstein

Again and again, the impossible problem is solved when we see that the problem is only a tough decision waiting to be made.

– Robert H. Schuller

I looked always outside of myself to see what I could make the world give me instead of looking within myself to see what was there.

– Belle Livingstone

If you are to be, you must begin by assuming responsibility. You alone are responsible for every moment of your life, for every one of your acts.

– Antoine de Saint Exupery

What counts is not necessarily the size of the dog in the fight; it's the size of the fight in the dog.

– Dwight D. Eisenhower

Perseverance is not a long race; it is many short races one after another.

– Walter Elliott

A mind troubled by doubt cannot focus on the course to victory.

– Arthur Golden

Optimism is the faith that leads to achievement. Nothing can be done without hope and confidence.

– Helen Keller

To gain that which is worth having, it may be necessary to lose everything else.

– Bernadette Devlin

Never talk defeat. Use words like hope, belief, faith, victory.

— Norman Vincent Peale

Character is like a tree and reputation like its shadow. The shadow is what we think of it; the tree is the real thing.

— Abraham Lincoln

The shortest and best way to make your fortune is to let people see clearly that it is in their interests to promote yours.

— Jean de La Bruyere

When you get to the end of your rope, tie a knot and hang on.

— Franklin D. Roosevelt

Your future takes precedence over your past. Focus on your future, rather than on the past.

— Gary Ryan Blair

Gratitude is the sign of noble souls.

— Aesop

Anyone who has never made a mistake has never tried anything new.

— Albert Einstein

When you believe and think "I can," you activate your motivation, commitment, confidence, concentration and excitement — all of which relate directly to achievement.

— Jerry Lynch

Things that are done, it is needless to speak about; things that are past, it is needless to blame.

— Confucius

It is difficulties that show what men are.

— Epictetus

He that can have patience can have what he will.

— Benjamin Franklin

Failure is the foundation of success; success is the lurking place of failure.

— Lao Tzu

All the world is searching for joy and happiness, but these cannot be purchased for any price in any market place, because they are virtues that come from within.

— Lucille R. Taylor

Drop the idea that you are Atlas carrying the world on your shoulders. The world would go on even without you. Don't take yourself so seriously.

— Norman Vincent Peale

Finally, I leave you with this old favorite of mine:

The Optimist Creed

I PROMISE MYSELF:

- To be so strong that nothing can disturb my peace of mind.
- To talk health, happiness, & prosperity to every person I meet.

- To make all my friends feel that there is something worthwhile in them.
- To look at the sunny side of everything & make my optimism come true.
- To think only of the best, to work only for the best, & to expect only the best.
- To be just as enthusiastic about the success of others as I am about my own.
- To forget the mistakes of the past and press on to the greater achievements of the future.
- To wear a cheerful expression at all times & give a smile to every living creature I meet.
- To give so much time to improving myself that I have no time to criticize others.
- To be too large for worry, too noble for anger, too strong for fear, & too happy to permit the presence of trouble.
- To think well of myself & to proclaim this fact to the world, not in loud word, but in great deeds.
- To live in the faith that the whole world is on my side, so long as I am true to the best that is in me.

Now go out and spread some positivity!

RESOURCE GUIDE

Go To: **http://www.TomMietzel.Com** For More Information and Free Gifts.

BOOKS ON LIFESTYLE REDESIGN

4 Hour Work Week – Timothy Ferris – Forget the old concept of retirement and the rest of the deferred-life-plan-there is no need to wait and every reason not to, especially in unpredictable economic times. Whether your dream is escaping the rat race, experiencing high-end world travel, earning a five-figure income with zero management, or just living more and working less, *The 4-Hour Workweek* is the blueprint.

Yes Energy – Loral Langemeier – The strongest energy always wins. That's it! That's the key to moving from your current situation, any situation, into the life you've always wanted. *Yes! Energy* presents the power of the "Energy Equation," which you can employ to attract abundance into your life. *Yes! Energy* can help you create the enterprise you've always envisioned; and dust off your dreams.

Rich Dad Poor Dad – Robert Kiyosaki – Anyone stuck in the rat-race of living paycheck to paycheck, enslaved by the house mortgage and bills, will appreciate this breath of fresh air. Learn about the methods that have created more than a few millionaires. Let Robert teach you how to think like a rich dad and let your money work for you!

Eat That Frog – Brian Tracy – So you want to get organized. You want to simplify your life. You want to learn to focus on priorities...to get more deals done in less time. The answer...read Brian Tracy's *Eat That Frog*.

DEBT ELIMINATION

The Total Money Makeover – Dave Ramsey – Ramsey debunks the many myths of money (exposing the dangers of cash advance, rent-to-own, debt consolidation) and attacks the illusions and downright deceptions of the American Dream, which encourages nothing but overspending and massive amounts of debt. "Don't even consider keeping up with the Joneses," Ramsey declares in his typically candid style. "They're broke!" *The Total Money Makeover* isn't theory. It works every single time. It works because it is simple. It works because it gets to the heart of your money problems: you.

CREDIT REPAIR

http://CreditNerds.com

REAL ESTATE TRAINING

Go to **http://www.TomMietzel.com** to work with our excellent trainers and coaches.

CD COURSES

http://www.nightingale.com (Bookmark this site as a resource for all your business and personal education and motivation)

The Missing Secret – Joe Vitale – Learn how to attract money, health, success, happiness, love and more into your life quickly, consistently and automatically, using the incredible power of the Law of Attraction PLUS the little known "Missing Secret" that opens the door to uninterrupted abundance. If the Law of Attraction isn't working for you all the time—or if you simply want to attract MORE—then this program is going to have an instant and astonishing impact on the results you are getting in life!

Wealth Magnet – Dr. Dolf de Roos – This is breakthrough information that's tested and measured – a system that can be applied by anyone. For instance, when Dolf de Roos, a successful real estate investor and author of the *Wealth Magnet* began teaching his real estate students the foundational beliefs that rich people share, his students' success rate went from 5 percent to over 80 percent!

The Wishes Fulfilled System – Dr. Wayne Dyer – Re-establish a cord of energy between your material self and the part of you that is part of the great fabric of God. Once you use your imagination to reconnect with your God-self, the road to manufacturing dreams with the right thought technology opens up before you.

Lead the Field – Earl Nightingale – Hundreds of thousands of people have profited from the wisdom and savvy of *Lead the Field*. In fact, it has often been referred to as the "Program of Presidents" because so many top executives have incorporated Earl's guidance and wisdom into their management philosophies.

The E Myth – Michael Gerber – Let Michael Gerber teach you how to work on your business, not in it, to create a perfect turnkey operation – a perfect money machine – that delivers predictable results, day after day, whether you are there or not.

The Secrets of Power Negotiating – Roger Dawson – Whether you are closing a major business deal or buying a new house, you have to be a negotiator every day. Let Roger Dawson teach you how to become a power negotiator so you can get anything you want!

Rich Dad Secrets – Robert Kiyosaki – The rich follow a different set of rules for making and keeping money. In fact, the rich live in a world most of us know nothing about. They pay less in taxes and set up their lives in such a way that money constantly flows to them

ABOUT TOM MIETZEL

Tom Mietzel knows more than just a thing or two about business. An entrepreneurial spirit, Mietzel kick-started his career in college and never looked back until the day his hard-earned success started to crumble. After a period of introspection and reflection, Mietzel recognized the value of his missteps and decided to share the lessons he learned.

Mietzel's success was overshadowed by the unexpected death of the woman he loved. Returning to work he found his businesses crumbling and his projects compromised. In 2007 Mietzel hit bottom, faced with lawsuits from former creditors, the emotional strain of the preceding few years, and his finances in tatters.

Mietzel's strong sense of faith and financial experiences helped him to recognize the value of the painful lessons he learned and put him on the road to recovery. A born leader, Mietzel decided to guide others down the road to recovery by sharing the good, the bad, and the ugly of his work, hoping to help and inspire other people who found themselves down and out.

Today, Mietzel continues to coach, train and motivate others in new business development and recovery from loss.

Claim Your **FREE** Gifts And Bonuses… A $97 Value For Book Buyers Only!

You'll receive:

- ✓ A free PDF of *The 14 Day Real Estate Investor – How To Buy Your First Small Investment Property*
- ✓ A free PDF of this book to share with your friends and family
- ✓ A Lifestyle Redesign Calculator…Learn how affordable your ideal life can be.

Learn how to let go of the past so you can live the incredible future you deserve.

Regardless of the source of your challenges and loss you can recover your self-esteem, rediscover your goals and passions and rebuild your business success.

Let Business and Life Coach Thomas Mietzel put you back on the path to success that is rightfully yours!

Get your free books and Lifestyle Redesign Calculator at:
http://www.TomMietzel.com

Made in the USA
Charleston, SC
06 December 2015